From Exile to Eden

· · · · · · ·

A Family Journal

JADWIGA SZELAZEK MORRISON

Illustrations by
Elizabeth Szelazek Emerson

TURNING
STONE
PRESS

First published in 2012 by
Turning Stone Press, an imprint of
Red Wheel/Weiser, LLC
With offices at:
665 Third Street, Suite 400
San Francisco, CA 94107
www.redwheelweiser.com

ISBN (paperback): 978-1-61852-040-1
ISBN (hardcover): 978-1-61852-039-5

Cover design by Jim Warner

Printed in the United States of America
IBT
10 9 8 7 6 5 4 3 2 1

This book is dedicated to the memory
of Tadeusz and Helena Szelazek . . .
two of the most extraordinary individuals I
have had the privilege of being related to.

Contents

Part I

The Ancestry, Legends, and Early Memories of the Szelazeks

⸙ 1 ⸙

November 20, 1918
Biala Podlaska, Lublin County, Poland

Saints Peter and Paul Cathedral in Lublin was as cold inside as it was outside, but the small crowd attending Helena Semerylo's christening was too focused on the happy event to think about the cold. The priest had just entered the date of birth on her baptismal certificate as November 20, 1918. It didn't matter that she was actually born on the 11th of November; many people used their baptismal date as their birthday. Lately, not many official birthdates were being registered in her county anyway. The war was the reason. So many towns were being burned to the ground—government buildings, records, and all.

Helena was born in the nearby village of Biala Podlaska (which translates to White Village near the Forest) where beautiful forests of white birch lined the road to town. These forests were now protecting all their loved ones. Out of these woods, the Polish Resistance continued their forays against the Austro-Germans who were moving through their villages and towns.

Helena's mom, Aniela, stood at the baptismal font and thought about the events of the past week. The fear she experienced would be permanently etched upon her memory. German soldiers were prowling through their village, ransacking their homes, and stealing all the supplies and food they could find as they slowly retreated back across Poland. This same scenario was being played out all over the country. The Central Powers were losing the war and the Austro-Germans were preparing to move their forces back. It was rumored that Charles the First, the last Hapsburg emperor, had abdicated on November 12th. That was the day after Helena had been born and it was also the day on which an Austrian soldier rounded up all the ducks and geese on the Semerylo property. The livestock and fowl were all the family had to keep them fed that winter. They would all certainly starve if no one stopped the looting.

That night, the commotion outside the farmhouse woke Aniela, who was alone with her new baby. Her husband had left earlier that day, at dawn, to go back into the forest to join the other Resistance fighters. Aniela slipped out of the house, leaving the one-day-old child sleeping in her crib. Unnoticed, she ran to the side of the house where a soldier had temporarily left the trussed birds. He was busy foraging through their barn, so he did not see her as she quickly cut the ropes that bound the fowl. She shooed the ducks and geese onto their large pond, hoping that it would be impossible for the soldier to retrieve the frightened birds from the water. This done, Aniela ran back into the house. As she lay on the bed with the baby next to her, her heart pounded from exertion and from the risk she was taking. The Austrian soldier soon became aware of what had happened to his loot. He burst

From Exile to Eden

into the bedroom, and as he pointed a gun at her, he cursed at her in a variety of languages.

"It was you who released the birds. I should kill you. If it weren't for this little baby next to you, you'd be dead. If I killed you, she'd die as well; and I don't kill babies. You should thank her for your life because she's the only reason you're still living!"

In the church, as she remembered this terrifying night, Aniela did thank God for being alive, for her two daughters, and for her husband Wladyslaw. God had been watching over them a lot lately. The Austro-German soldiers had nearly caught Wladyslaw on several occasions. He was a commandant in the Polish Volunteer Army (Polska Ochotnicza Wojsko—it was this army that later pushed back the Bolsheviks as they tried to take over eastern Poland). The battles in Poland never seemed to end; just living was a constant battle for the Polish people. If it wasn't war, it was starvation, or sickness, and Aniela was weary of it all.

On this day, the whole Semerylo family was in the church, attending the christening of Helena. The officiating priest wasn't the one Aniela had expected to perform the service. They had requested Father Sliwonji, who was a relative of hers, but he had recently been executed by the Austro-German soldiers for spying.

Father Sliwonji had been in the church bell tower, with binoculars, watching the advance of the soldiers, and he had sent word to the Polish Resistance of the enemy's location. Unfortunately, the Germans had seen a glint of light reflected from his binoculars as he hid in the tower. When they could find no other people in the church, the Germans dragged him out and shot him. They hadn't seen the man running toward the forests with news of the

German approach. The civilians had been warned and the Resistance was ready.

In the cathedral, everyone spoke in hushed voices, remembering the many good deeds of the brave priest. When they prayed that day, they prayed for him as well as their own families. Father Sliwonji met his end with courage and defiance. His parishioners, in this small ravaged town, wondered if they would also meet the same fate as the war dragged on.

⁀ 2 ⁀

November 20, 1918
Stannowo, Nieszawa,
Warsaw County, Poland

His breath left steamy gray circles on the glass panes as he looked out on the gardens ravaged by frost. Those once fragrant, gloriously brilliant blooms and luxuriant bushes were now dark, blighted ruins. No longer did anyone stop to stare in amazement, as they had this past summer when everything had been a wild mass of color. There were so many unusual plants growing in their ornamental gardens; plants that some people had never seen before—except in books. The little boy drew circles on the steamy cloud covering the window. He dreaded the coming of winter, which was already leaving its mark on the flowerbeds. His mother, Antonina Zalewska Szelazek, had lovingly planted the gardens years ago, and they had been a constant source of joy for her. Not that there was much joy these days, what with the war dragging on the way it had. And what a war it was! So many people dead, so much damage and suffering!

"Why are some people calling this the Great War, father?" the boy asked.

His father looked up from the ledgers on his desk.

"Maybe it is a 'great' war, but it's just another war for the Polish people. It seems that wars in Europe always involve us in some way. Don't you have anything to do, Tadeusz, besides asking me questions all morning long? I've never heard a more talkative nine-year-old. Your brothers and sisters can answer your questions. Go bother them."

Franciszek pretended to be annoyed by his son's inquisitive nature but was obviously proud of his son's intelligent, questioning mind. Tadeusz had been born on July 26, 1909, and was the eighth of his nine children. This one resembled him in many ways. The blonde-haired, blue-eyed boy continued to gaze questioningly at his father. His thin face wore a determined, concerned gaze. Questions demanded answers and Tadeusz seldom failed to get them. This boy of his should do well in the future, if he lived long enough, Franciszek thought. He continued to review the household accounts as his son resumed his questioning.

"I just want to know when the war will be over."

"The armistice was signed nine days ago, but that doesn't mean that the fighting will stop."

"Is everything going to be okay now?"

"I'm not a psychic, so I can't answer that. I just don't know. Our country has been partitioned for too long and I'm worried that our sense of national unity is gone. There hasn't been a Polish nation in over 100 years. Germans and Russians are roaming the countryside, taking whatever is in their path. Our Polish people are still being forced to fight brother against brother, depending on which portion of the country they're living in and which army has forced them into service. We are being systematically murdered while other nations are saying the war's over. Eight months ago the (Russian) Tsar's army signed a peace treaty with the Germans and then pulled out of the war when the world needed them most. Now the Tsar and his family are dead and the new leaders are calling themselves Bolsheviks. Comrade Lenin is running the Russian government. Some of the Russians left for home when they signed the treaty, but then the Bolsheviks decided they should keep control of Russian Poland. The Treaty of Brest-Litovsk has only caused fighting among the Bolsheviks. The world may be calling our country the Republic of Poland, but we're not free yet. Some of our Polish Resistance fighters are still battling with both the Russians and the Germans, as we speak. I wish we could keep them out of Poland forever."

"So, what you're saying is that the war is over, but it's not, right?"

"Probably not for a while . . . . Now that the Russian Bolsheviks are in power, we'll start seeing changes soon enough. Perhaps they'll liberate some of our household belongings the way the Germans have."

Tadeusz looked around at their comfortable home. He imagined it being "liberated" by Bolshevik soldiers and wondered what they'd take and what they'd destroy. Periodic German occupation of his household over the years had resulted in sparse furnishings. However, his home still had some nice pieces of furniture, and his parents' upper class status showed in them. Their house was the nicest one in the area and he was glad he had been born there. The building's construction was good enough to last a few centuries if need be. The outside walls were made of white-painted stucco. The house and the other structures on the property were surrounded by gardens, several acres of forests, and fields for farming. All of it belonged to them, the Szelazeks. At least it had remained theirs through this war, and maybe it would get through this new Bolshevik problem as well.

"How will our country be treated by the Russians now that we are independent?"

"They'll treat us the way they always had, as a weaker neighbor who can be pushed around."

On June 3, 1918, the world powers had declared Poland an entity. They were to be liberated by the Allies, and Poland was now considered an independent nation. Tadeusz remembered the celebration they threw on July 4th. His parents had celebrated that day, as had their Polish countrymen, announcing their independence. It had seemed an extremely appropriate date for an Independence Day celebration. The Americans were celebrating their Independence Day along with the Poles. It was a wonderful day; and, fortunately for them, most of their family was alive and present for the celebration.

Tadeusz thought about his family and how they had come to be called Szelazek.

"Father, why do you call great-grandfather Lord Zielinski and not Lord Szelazek like everyone else?"

He liked hearing the story and Franciszek began retelling the old family history.

Zielinski had been a freeman of good lineage who ran the estates of an earl (hrabia). He was the chief administrator: he kept all the accounts and supervised the running of the entire village that belonged to the earl. The earl's son was studying at the Sorbonne in Paris when the old earl died and left the entire estate to his son. The newly titled earl arrived home and began a life of grand excesses—booze, women, gambling. Everyone knew that, if he continued at this rate, he would soon run through the inheritance and put the entire estate into jeopardy. The situation came to a head one day while the young great-grandfather Zielinski was looking over a pair of workhorses with the new earl.

Apparently, the new heir was talking about his plans to sell these workhorses and to purchase some racehorses in their place. This would mean the existing stables would need to be expanded and a great deal of money would need to be spent. This blatant extravagance was something to which Zielinski was vehemently opposed. He tried to reason with the young man, explaining how it was the earl's responsibility to look after the people who were in service to him. The serfs needed workhorses to plough the fields, not racehorses for entertainment. The earl had already squandered so much money that the threat of bankruptcy in their future was quite real. The serfs couldn't pay any more taxes and the estate's expenses were exceeding its income. The new earl objected to being lectured by Zielinski about his finances. To make matters worse, Zielinski was a fairly young man at the time. If the earl were to be lectured, he would have preferred to have someone older (and his social equal) doing the lecturing. He was infuriated by this serious, capable, young administrator who was so different from him.

"You're just a paid servant. Who do you think you are, telling me what to do?"

With that, he slapped Zielinski in the face and tried to use a horse whip on him. That was the wrong thing to do. No one dishonored the Zielinski name and got away with it. Family honor demanded satisfaction. However, waiting for satisfaction by way of a duel, would take too long . . . particularly if one was being whipped in the meantime. So, Zielinski defended himself by grabbing some chains (which were used to control the horses) and beating up the supercilious earl. Zielinski then ordered the grooms to hitch up a team of four (of the earl's best horses) to a carriage. He made a quick stop at his home where his manservant packed their belongings, and drove them into Prussian territories. There he set up a new life for himself, believing that he must surely have killed the earl. He gave his manservant the name of Psiarski (a name that emphasized the servant's faithfulness and companionship, like a faithful dog). He gave himself the name of Szelazek, a derivative of szelag, a coin of the times worth two pence or one shilling. This was a fitting name because he had always been good with money and investments. His choice of the new name was an interesting play on words. Zielinski meant greenery, vegetation, or weeds, while the word Szelazek also meant a type of common, rapid-spreading weed or plant. In this way, Zielinski kept the basic meaning of his name.

Zielinski bought a large estate in Prussia, and with his quick wit and financial savvy, he soon made himself a fortune. He bought himself a title and became Lord Szelazek. He gave his servant, Psiarski, his freedom as well as a small income to support his new status as a freeman. The new Lord Szelazek had always believed in the equality of all men, and he disliked the feudal treatment of the serfs in Poland. He admired the beliefs of Tadeusz Kosciuszko who advocated freeing all slaves—American slaves as well as Polish serfs.

As the young Tadeusz listened to this tale, his father told him that he was named after that Polish freedom fighter. Tadeusz Kosciuszko was a hero in Polish history as well as in the American Revolution. (Later in his own life, Tadeusz Szelazek would have the opportunity to drink vodka with the great grandnephew of Tadeusz Kosciuszko.) His father then continued the tale.

News of home was eventually brought to Zielinski/Szelazek. He was informed that the young earl did not die from the beating. The earl had, apparently, realized the error of his extravagant ways after he nearly bankrupted his estate and lost most of his inheritance. So, when the earl found out where Szelazek was living, he sent a messenger offering him a pardon. The earl asked Szelazek to come back and work for him again. Lord Szelazek accepted the pardon but told the earl that he would never work for anyone ever again.

This offer of a pardon might also have been timed with the formation of the new Polish constitution. The newly formed government was offering pardons to any expatriated Polish citizens living in foreign countries. They were being pardoned for any previous misdeeds that kept them from returning to their newly liberated country. After selling off everything in Prussia, Szelazek returned to Poland where he married and settled in Kujawa. The fortune and title he brought back assured his family's comfort for a long, long time.

The tale ended and Franciszek went back to work on the ledgers. Through the window, Tadeusz watched two of his brothers walk a matched pair of Arabian stallions near the stables.

"Did your cousin, Adolf Szelazek, give you those horses, Father?"

"Yes, he did, son."

Adolf Szelazek, one of Lord Zielinski's grandsons (born August 1, 1865), was a Catholic priest who would eventually become the Bishop of the Lodz diocese. As was the custom in those days, the eldest son inherited the estate and title, while the younger sons became soldiers or priests. Adolf, although wealthy in his own right, decided to enter the clergy. He was a generous, intelligent, creative member of the Szelazek family. As a member of the Polish delegation, Adolf would eventually become famous for negotiating the Bolshevik Treaty of Riga, Latvia, in 1921. In addition, his work with Prince Janusz Radziwil, who was the minister of Foreign Affairs, would lead to the Concordat in Riga. (A *concordat* is an agreement between the Roman Catholic Church and a secular government on matters that concern the church in that country.) He would also go on to write several books and papers on church and secular themes. Bishop Adolf would eventually die at his home in the Palace Bierzglow on February 9, 1950, and would be buried at St. Jacob's Church in Torun.

"Those horses must be the fastest animals in the world!" Tadeusz interjected into Franciszek's thoughts.

With this comment, Franciszek remembered how the highly spirited animals wrecked an expensive carriage just recently. To call the Arabian stallions "fast" was an understatement. Their feet barely touched the ground as they ran. The horses seemed to enjoy racing the train, following the tracks that lay alongside the country road that lead toward town. One day, during a trip into town, they were in a particularly energetic mood when the reins broke. Once given free rein, they broke into a gallop that shattered the carriage in half. They dragged the remaining portion in circles around a field until Franciszek could stop them. (At that moment, no one could have guessed that, within the year, those stallions would be stolen by thieves. Franciszek would enter the stables when the actual theft was occurring. He would be hit on the head with a shovel and left unconscious. The valuable stallions would never be recovered; but Franciszek would be lucky that they did not kill and rob him.)

"Tell me about mother's side of the family."

"Well, Antonina's maternal great, great grandmother had land holdings in Plowiec, which had been their property since at least the time of King Wladyslaw Lokietek (1306–1333). Your mother was three when her mother died. Her father was so devastated that he died of a heart attack almost immediately after his wife's death. So, your mother was basically an orphan.

Antonina was from the old aristocracy (nobility) and was, therefore, well off. She should have inherited 10,000 gold rubles. This money would have been the equivalent of 500 head of cattle, which was a large amount at that time. With Antonina's father dead, her uncles (her mother's brothers) became her legal guardians. They figured out a way to cheat her out of her inheritance since they had complete control over all her finances. The uncles devised a plan to marry her off to someone of the 'landed gentry' status. The dowry could be smaller if her suitor was from a lower social class. Their plan was to withhold as much of the dowry as possible and to keep it for themselves. If they played their cards right, they could renege on their part of the marriage agreement completely.

They assumed that if she married a lord or nobleman, they would be forced to pay the expected large dowry that went along with the marriage. A lord would expect her entire inheritance and would have the legal connections (power) to get his due. So they thought they would be clever and marry her off to someone 'more common.' They didn't count on her marrying someone like me!"

Franciszek had taken the uncles to court and had won the lawsuit. He received the money for her dowry; however, it was all in paper and not in gold coin. When the Great War (WWI) erupted, the paper money lost its value and the currency became worthless. Tadeusz had seen how some people actually used the paper money to wallpaper their walls and used it as fire kindling in their stoves.

"When you and mother found out that they weren't going to give you the dowry, did you *really* pay her uncles a visit with your shotgun laid across your arm? You must have impressed them with the fact that you meant business. Great-grandfather Zielinski would have been proud of you, Dad!"

"Are you finished with all the questions, Tadeusz? I don't know who is more annoying, you or your brother Roman. He has certainly caused us serious grief lately."

Recently, the Germans had quartered soldiers in their house. Roman had been extremely angered with the way the Germans had made themselves at home with all their possessions. Being young (18), headstrong, patriotic, and foolish, he decided to show his displeasure with the situation. The soldiers had gone off on patrol when Roman went into their room and defecated upon one of the beds. He then collected some of their weapons and belongings, dropped them into the well in the courtyard, and then he left home. Roman ran off and joined the Polish Resistance. He had not considered the effect of his actions upon the rest of the family. The German soldiers were furious. They immediately wanted to kill the entire family on the spot; but his mother Antonina had cried, begged, and apologized till the Germans relented.

In the meantime, Roman became a volunteer in the Polish Legion and even went on to become a secretary to General Wladyslaw Anders. Roman's handwriting was excellent, so it was no surprise to the family that he became a secretary to such a distinguished military man. What did surprise them was Roman's subsequent reckless behavior. He had joined the army to fight the Germans. So, instead of enjoying his safe, cushy job with the General, he hated it. It wasn't long before he took off (without permission) to the front lines. During one particularly bloody battle, General Anders spotted him among the soldiers and asked him what he was doing there. Apparently, he liked the young man's courage and determination and, consequently, didn't turn him in to stand court-martial. When the war eventually ended, Roman was offered land as payment for his efforts in the war. He refused the offer saying that he had fought for his country and not for profit. Not many people were that idealistic.

☙ 3 ❧

Summer 1920
Biala Podlaska, Lublin County,
Poland

Bolshevik soldiers called the "Corpse's Skull Regiment" were raiding the countryside, "liberating" everyone's livestock and valuables. There was famine in Russia and food was as important as territory. The Treaty of Versailles (June 1919) had granted Poland a narrow belt of territory extending along the Vistula River to the Baltic Sea and large sections of Poznan and West Prussia. It was over these lands and property that soldiers from the Russian Red Guard were now fighting the newly formed Republic of Poland. The Premier, Ignacy Paderewski, ordered the Polish armies to invade the Ukraine and put an end to all the fighting.

The area was being shelled and none of the villagers were safe. Wladyslaw Semerylo was fighting the Bolsheviks with as much determination as he had the Germans. He struck at the enemy when they least expected it, retreating to the safety of the forests where he joined up with the other men of his village. They had to be careful, and they had to be especially wary of the residents

18

of Russian descent. Although none of the Byelorussians liked being shelled and bullied about by soldiers, they could still prove traitorous. The men of the Polish Resistance knew they had to be cautious.

Wladyslaw tried to come home whenever possible, but he was away on the day that Aniela heard the Bolsheviks coming. She grabbed her two daughters and their best milking cow and made her way into the nearby forest. Her eldest daughter, Stasia, was four and a half and Helena was one and a half. Aniela knew her livestock would be destroyed, but if she could save the cow, at least her children wouldn't starve to death.

The Russian soldiers were burning down the village and driving the farm animals into the river where they were shot or drowned. The Bolsheviks were determined to leave nothing that the Polish armies, or the civilian Polish Resistance, could use as food or shelter. It didn't matter to the Russians that they were destroying the lives of the Polish villagers, as well as some of their own people. The soldiers had already burned down 180 houses when Aniela heard them coming. The village would be completely destroyed that day . . . all except for the school and the church (which were on opposite sides of the village). Aniela turned to see her beautiful home burst into flames. Wladyslaw had built the large, eight-room building soon after they were married, and now it would be burned down like kindling. She, and all the devastated villagers, would soon be forced to sleep in the only two remaining buildings of their burned-out village.

At least there would be milk for the children, even if everything else were taken, she thought. She pulled at the terrified cow and headed toward the tree line of the forest. Aniela held onto Helena with one arm while

Stasia held onto her skirt for dear life. Once they made the safety of the forest, they hid themselves in a ditch behind some dense bushes. As they prepared to spend the night there, she prayed for the safety of their family. Fear, sorrow, and eventually exhaustion, overcame her and she fell asleep.

An overwhelming feeling of danger awakened her. She knew that she had to move from the spot where she was lying. Quickly she moved herself and the girls to an area not far from the ditch. Within minutes a shell dropped and exploded on the very spot they had just moved from. They would have been dead, blown to bits, if she had not heeded the urgent warning in her head. Her guardian angel was working overtime.

Sleep was no longer possible. Aniela waited for dawn and some sign of ceasing activity in the burned-out village. She had lots of time to think as she waited for peace to return to her little corner of the world. She thought about her husband, Wladyslaw.

Wladyslaw had been born on September 8, 1889 to Bartlomiej and Anna Semerylo, who had a small, rather poor estate. As a teenager, he took a job working on the estate of a wealthy woman; as a result, he probably had more independence and freedom than most boys did at his age. At 18, he began traveling around the world looking for work and adventure. He left for America and eventually found construction work in Buffalo, New York. Then he moved on to Chicago, Illinois, where he worked on road construction and other odd jobs. When he returned to Poland, after spending six years abroad, he met Aniela Kosieracka. He was a 24-year-old worldly traveler when he married 16-year-old Aniela. The wedding festivities lasted for four days and had everyone talking about their lavishness. Wladyslaw had brought home most of the earnings from his travels and the newly married couple was able to buy a good piece of land with it. The house was built, livestock was bought, and equipment was purchased. Soon they began farming the land.

Wladyslaw's father, Bartlomiej Semerylo, could not understand why his son would prefer wandering the globe like some fortune hunter to staying at home and working such a neat, productive farm. And yet, it was obvious that the domesticated life of a farmer was not what Wladyslaw yearned for. He had inherited a gypsy spirit from some ancestor (some suspected that Mongol blood ran in his veins), and he preferred travel to a calm, settled life. Even war held more fascination for Wladyslaw than farming did. However, he worked hard when he had to, fought hard, and played hard. It was Wladyslaw's adventurous spirit that made life interesting and exciting—sometimes too exciting.

Wladyslaw made an excellent soldier because of his courage, quick thinking, and bravery. He was considered a local hero during the Great War (WWI) when he commanded the local militia. They were able to repel the Germans as they tried to reorganize their army near Biala Podlaska. He had received a silver medal from the newly formed Polish government for that encounter with the enemy. In later years, a Russian Communist official in the "new" Polish government (after WWII) stole this medal from him. She said she needed to register his medals and accomplishments since they could result in a higher pension when he retired. At her insistence, Wladyslaw left the medal with her at the local NKVD (Narodnyi

Komisariat Vnutrennikh Dyel—the Russian Security Police) office. He never saw his medal again. The NKVD conveniently lost it.

Aniela knew how brave and resourceful her husband was. She remembered the story he told about the time he was nearly caught by some Bolshevik soldiers as he was making his way home. It was dark when he left the other Polish Resistance fighters in the forest. He carefully made his way home to check on the family and was already close to the back steps of his home when a Russian soldier spotted him. The soldier was on horseback and Wladyslaw was on foot, but he decided to run toward the trees and draw the soldier away from his home. He ducked behind a bush, dropped his revolver in a shallow depression, and covered it with leaves. Then he proceeded to drop his pants and defecate on top of the spot where the revolver was hidden. The soldier saw what looked like a man suffering from a bad case of stomach troubles. It appeared that the poor farmer must have had a bad attack in the middle of the night and never made it to the outhouse, which was standing close by. Fortunately for Wladyslaw, he was actually able to produce a bowel movement with which to conceal his weapon. No one would bother moving the stool around to search for anything on the ground. So, after his clothes were searched for weapons, the soldier let him go. Later he was able to go back and retrieve the revolver covered with its "silent witness." Quick thinking, and a bowel movement, had saved his life.

∽ 4 ∽

Summer 1920
Stannowo, Nieszawa, Warsaw
County, Poland

Tadeusz was 11 and was out hunting for birds. Perhaps he'd find a falcon again. He still remembered how much it hurt when the mother falcon attacked him as he climbed the steep cliff toward the nest. He got her chick out of the nest and trained it, just like the professional falconers did. Birds were his first love and he knew all of them by name, sight, and song. He seemed to spend more time in the trees than on the ground. His yard was filled with pheasants, trained homing pigeons, and other birds. Today, however, there were few birds around and he'd have to settle for making the lives of barn swallows miserable.

He loved catching swallows in the barn. It was more than just the fun of catching the little birds that fascinated him. He and his brothers would also cook them and eat them. There wasn't much meat on swallows, but the boys considered them a delicacy. Perhaps it was more the joy of catching a meal than the actual taste of swallows that made the hunt so important. His brother Leon often accompanied him up into the rafters where the two boys would lie in wait for the unsuspecting birds. They would take turns poking the birds off the rafters and scooping them up in a net. Unfortunately, Leon was not as agile or athletic as Tadeusz, so he rarely caught anything.

Tadeusz would roust a bird from its perch.

"Masz?" (Did you get him?)

Leon would answer in his unsophisticated, country drawl.

"Ucik." (He got away.)

This infuriated Tadeusz on a number of levels. First of all, the word was Uciek, not Ucik. Using the improper pronunciation smacked of laziness, ignorance, and social inferiority. These were vices that Tadeusz tried to avoid throughout his life. His constant endeavors to perfect his language and social graces held him in good stead over the years to come. He had always prided himself in his correct usage of the Polish language and he believed it was criminal to destroy or alter it. (For years, the Polish language had to be studied secretly since it had been forbidden by the Russians and Germans to be spoken publicly.) His brother Leon, however, could care less about education or the proper pronunciation of words. This lazy attitude was bad enough, but what infuriated Tadeusz even more was his brother's total lack of coordination and hunting skills.

After the fifth attempt to catch a bird, Tadeusz couldn't stand to hear another "Ucik," so he poked his brother with the pole, knocking him out of the rafters down onto a pile of hay on the barn floor. Of course his brother squealed on him. Tadeusz got a scolding and the mandatory beating, which he bore resolutely and not without some satisfaction. It almost seemed worth the beating to see his brother fly through the air like the birds he couldn't catch.

∼ 5 ∼

Summer 1922
Biala Podlaska, Lublin County, Poland

Helena Semerylo was nearly four when they told her that her favorite grandfather, Kosieracki, was dying. She was too frightened to be near him and it was the fault of all those adults around her. They thought that telling those ridiculous ghost stories was fun; and the Grim Reaper was an especially good story with which to terrify small children. She was afraid the Reaper would accidentally cut her head off when he was coming for her grandfather. Helena was torn between the desire to see her beloved grandfather and her fear to be anywhere nearby. There was nothing that she could do to protect herself and grandfather if the Reaper was in the room. They told her to bring some milk to her grandfather Kosieracki, but she could not carry it to him because of her overwhelming fear. The adults around her were too preoccupied to pay any attention to her. They had no idea of the turmoil going on within her. Her mother, Aniela, and the others were upset, but she was devastated.

Aniela, born on January 6, 1897, was one of three children born to Piotr (Peter) Kosieracki. Aniela's mother (Rosalia Trebicki) had first been married to a man named Jozef Buczynski with whom she had two children, Jozef and Maria (Maria died at the age of 18). Rosalia's husband Buczynski died and she then married Piotr Kosieracki. It was a marriage that cost Rosalia her sister's love. Her sister had had her sights set on the handsome Piotr, but she never dreamed that the man would prefer a widow to her. But it turned out that he did prefer the widowed Rosalia with her two children. When the couple got married, her sister left the family home and took up with a radical, bogus, religious sect (The Kozlowity). Piotr Kosieracki was a good father to the two stepchildren as well as to his own three children. The three Kosieracki children were Anna (married Maslewski), Bronislawa (married Brodacki), and Aniela (married Wladyslaw Semerylo).

Piotr Kosieracki was an educated man who had over 300 books in his home. People would borrow books from him as though he were the local librarian. He never begrudged anyone access to books or knowledge. Unfortunately, some of the villagers had no respect for the knowledge within the books. They would rip out pages to use as cigarette papers whenever there was a shortage of paper.

Kosieracki also gave religious instructions, held catechism classes, and taught Polish to the village children. The Russians had burned down the church in his village, so he used his home as a school. Piotr Kosieracki had started the practice of instructing children years ago when Poland had been under Russian and Prussian domination. Then, teaching Polish was punishable by deportation to Siberia, but Kosieracki insisted that it would be death for Poland if the language and traditions were not continued. He felt it was his duty to his country to teach it to the children. The threat of death and torture didn't frighten him as much as it did other people, or if it did, he didn't let it get in his way.

Piotr Kosieracki was a stubborn, dedicated, brave man who knew what torture felt like. It was German soldiers who had broken his health and brought him to this, the day of his death. The Great War was raging around them when the Germans came looking for his stepson, Jozef Buczynski. They accused Jozef of storing hidden weapons that were being used by the Polish Resistance. Piotr Kosieracki had been questioned in German as to his stepson's location. He didn't know how to speak German, only a few select phrases. So he told them, "Nicht sprechen Deutsche." Unfortunately, answering them in German made them angry. They insisted that he could speak German if he was able to answer them with a German phrase. They beat him with a rifle, then tied him to a horse and dragged him around the yard. His lungs and internal organs were injured and this was what caused him to die prematurely.

A few days later, Helena looked at her grandmother, Rosalia Kosieracki, during her second husband's funeral. She thought she was the most beautiful lady in the world. Sometimes, in church, Helena would watch her grandmother's face and compare her to all the other grandmothers. In the little girl's eyes, there was no comparison.

Her grandmother Rosalia had come from a place called Chluszcza Wiski, Tucznia. She had been part of the old aristocracy, the Szlachta Zasciankowa (Nobility behind the Wall). The aristocracy was usually extended many privileges, but there was also a family story about Rosalia's father and taxes.

Their family had been exempt from taxes because of Rosalia's father, who had served in Tadeusz Kosciuszko's army (1794). He repaid those who were loyal to him and who had served with him in the Polish Army. Great Grandfather Trebicki had received a title, money, land, and four white horses that were kept for show in ceremonies and on special occasions. These horses stood as a symbol of his patriotism and his fighting spirit. Polish Independence never became a reality in his lifetime, but that never stopped him or any Pole from trying to gain it.

⌒ 6 ⌒

1922–1927
Biala Podlaska,
Lublin County, Poland

By 1922, things were more calm in Poland . . . calm, but not peaceful. Political factions were fighting; the economic and political rights of the people (particularly the minorities) were not being protected; and Poland was a nation in financial crisis. When the need for money arose again, Wladyslaw left home for a period of five years to earn money abroad. This time, however, he was not a carefree bachelor roaming the world. At the time of his departure, his daughter Stasia was six-and-a-half while Helena was four; Aniela was pregnant with their son, Kazio (Casmir).

This time he headed for South America and worked in Buenos Aires, Argentina. It was in Argentina that he had the opportunity to travel widely, observing and studying some of the strange local practices. There was a lot to take in—voodoo, black magic rituals, zombies, and supernatural beliefs he had never encountered before. He saw how some natives took revenge upon their enemies by using effigies of the living victims and focusing their energies on them. Wladyslaw tried to learn everything he could while he was there. His experiences gave him a broader appreciation of the powers of the mind and a glimpse into the unexplained phenomena that exist. His travels broadened his outlook on life.

When he eventually returned to Poland, Wladyslaw found himself treated like a native Marco Polo. He would sit on the front porch and thrill the children of the village with his descriptions of the world. He would take them into a far-off world inhabited by strange people with strange powers. In the summer, people would gather on his porch and ask him to repeat the same stories over and over again. These tales influenced Helena greatly. She realized that the world was a huge, diverse, exciting experience waiting to happen.

However, it was 1927 before Wladyslaw returned to his home and family. An awful lot of history would happen during his absence—Jozef Pilsudski would be running an independent Poland, Helena would be eight and a very different child from when he left, her sister Stasia would be ten, and her brother Kazio (who was born after he left in 1922) should have been five years old. Unfortunately, Wladyslaw never got the opportunity to see his son alive.

Summer 1925

Seven-year-old Helena had been sitting up against a low stone fence, feeding her three-year-old brother, when her uncle came by to inspect the crops in the adjacent field. He saw a stray cow chewing up some of the newly planted seedlings and became enraged. He struck the cow on its rump. The startled beast took off at a gallop and attempted to jump the stone fence. It got hung up and

Helena, Aniela, Kazio, and Stasia Semerylo

was straddled across it when Jozef Buczynski caught up to it. Unfortunately, Helena was directly behind the fence precisely where the cow had decided to jump. Now she was caught between the cow's front legs and the stone fence. Uncle Buczynski, unaware of the girl's presence, kept beating the cow to get it off the fence while it kept kicking Helena on the back of her head with its hoof. It cracked her skull and pushed in a small section of the cracked bone, indenting her skull.

She was lying with her head in a pool of blood when they found her. The screams of her brother Kazio, whom she had pushed away to safety, were what finally alerted everyone to the horrible accident. Her mother and uncle patched up Helena's head as best as they could. They lived too far away from a hospital to get help. There were no doctors in the area, and they couldn't afford one any-way. Miraculously, she lived. The damage to her skull, however, caused Helena severe migraines for many years. Eventually, as she grew older, the headaches subsided, but the small flattened area on her skull remained as a reminder of that day.

It seems that unfortunate accidents kept happening to Helena throughout her life. At the age of four, and then again as a teenager, she was hit by lightening. The first strike happened when she sat upon her father's knee as he drove a team of horses. The lightning struck the lead horse, killing it instantly; it then traveled up the reins and hit both her and her father. The second time, she was standing in the doorway of the barn when light-ning struck the ground near her and threw her across the room. She, fortunately, did not sustain any serious inju-ries, but thunderstorms became a lifelong fear of hers.

However, there was a positive side to all of these accidents. By the time Helena reached the age of seven, she started demonstrating various psychic abilities that the family strove to keep secret. These psychic abilities played a great role in her future life, and in the lives of her family. It seems that life-threatening accidents and traumatic illnesses often trigger increased psychic abilities. This was definitely the case with Helena. Her life was no longer ordinary.

1927

In 1927, a sudden outbreak of diphtheria devastated the surrounding district. The disease killed young and old alike. Competent, certified doctors usually charged 100 zloty for a visit (for comparison, a cow could be purchased for 80 zloty). Not many could afford such an expense in 1927, so most villagers called in "healers" to treat their children. These so-called healers still used primitive methods like bloodletting and leaches. As a result, many victims died from the treatments they received from some of these uneducated practitioners. When the schoolteacher's child contracted diphtheria, he called in a real doctor, however. He was one of the few people with an income sufficient to pay for the doctor's services. Aniela Semerylo approached the doctor on his way out of the teacher's home and begged him to save her daughter, Helena, who was grievously ill with the disease. She was choking as a result of the lesions and swelling in her throat. The doctor agreed and swabbed Helena's throat with some kind of medicine (he called it lapis). It caused the throat lesions to burst open, pushing out the fluid and pus, which she immediately vomited out. The swelling went down as soon as the lesions were drained, allowing her to breathe better. The doctor had saved her life. Unfortunately, it was too late for her younger brother, Kazio, who had died the week before.

Keeping with the funerary customs of the day, little Kazio's body was laid out in the house. The family would keep vigil over it for three days. His body would then be buried on the third day. This was an unbearable heart-break for Helena. Her beloved brother had died. She had been more of a mother to him than a sister since she had been taking care of him for most of his life. Kazio had called her his "Helcia" and it was to her that he turned when he needed comforting. Aniela had been too busy trying to run the farm single-handedly in Wladyslaw's absence; the family's livelihood and survival was her responsibility. While keeping vigil, Helena fell asleep resting her head near Kazio's body. She was exhausted from crying and her throat was beginning to hurt. It was the first sign of diphtheria and she knew it would soon be her turn to be ill, and perhaps die like her brother. The last thing she remembered before she fell asleep was asking God why Kazio had to die. If someone had to die, she would rather it had been her. As she slept, she felt that this sleep was somehow different from her usual unconscious state. She felt herself leaving her body and moving along a path of brilliant light through a peaceful, beautiful landscape. She saw her brother walking down the road, through a breathtakingly beautiful land covered with strange colorful flowers and shrubs.

"Kazio, come back! Mama will be sad if you leave us."

"I can't, I have to go to Bozia (God) now."

Helena started to cry and reached out toward him.

"Please, at least take a sweater with you so you won't be cold."

He gave a delighted laugh at that.

"Don't cry, Helcia. I'm not cold here. It doesn't hurt anymore. Really! It's beautiful here and I'm happy, but I will miss you and wish I could be with you."

"Then I'll stay here with you. I don't want to live without you. I love you."

"No, you have to go back. You have to take care of mother. You have to live. I love you."

Helena came awake with a start as his form faded away before her eyes. And there, on the table, was Kazio's dead little body. She was feeling stiff, hot, and more dead than alive, and her heart was breaking from the loss of her brother. She cried harder than ever, waking her mother and sister from their exhausted sleep.

~

Wladyslaw returned two months after Kazio's death. He was upset that his son had died while he was away and somehow he blamed his wife for not taking better care of the children. Sometimes people can be cruel and insensitive when grief takes them over the edge. Wladyslaw had always wanted a son, and now it seemed he would never have one. It was a sad homecoming.

There were also other disappointments. Wladyslaw had brought back very little money this time. It wasn't like his previous moneymaking expeditions. Money was scarce throughout all of Europe. Actually, most of the world was in pretty bad shape economically. Germany was suffering a major financial depression and Hitler was making everyone aware of it at the Nuremberg Rally. Long before the U.S. experienced the Great Depression, which began in 1929, Poland was experiencing an ongoing depression. But because Poland's economy had been in a poor state for decades, any new declines were less devastating for them than for other foreign countries.

Wladyslaw did manage to bring home some gifts from his travels in North and South America, however. He brought back eight oranges, which he divided between

Stasia and Helena. However, Stasia tricked Helena into giving up her oranges. Stasia knew that the peel of the orange had to be removed since it was not meant to be bitten into, like an apple. However, Helena had never seen an orange before and was easily fooled. Stasia told her to take a big bite, which Helena did; she grimaced from the awful, bitter-tasting fruit and gave her remaining oranges to Stasia. It was a dirty trick, but that was typical of Stasia. Stasia quickly hid in the closet, with all of the oranges, and proceeded to gorge herself. There was only one orange left when Wladyslaw noticed that Helena was not eating any of the fruit. He scolded Stasia for being such a greedy, conniving, mean-spirited glutton.

The scolding didn't really help since it was Stasia's nature to be greedy and sneaky. She was always adept at creating trouble if there was any profit in it for her. As a matter of fact, it didn't take long for her to get into more trouble. She took one of the expensive Argentinean shawls Wladyslaw had brought back for his wife, and cut it up to make dolls' dresses. She constantly gave into any temptation that struck her fancy at the time, regardless of the hurt doing so inflicted upon others. Age and experience never did change her selfish outlook on life.

~ 7 ~

1927
Stannowo, Nieszawa, Warsaw
County, Poland

Tadeusz, a young man of 18, was trying his hand at
whatever job opportunities and skills he could find.
He took business courses to prepare himself for clerking
and bookkeeping. He dreamed of owning his own store,
and he saved whatever he could with this goal in mind.
Money was tight and his parents were struggling to keep
the estate solvent. He knew he couldn't depend on financial help from anyone, with the exception of an older
married sister, Wladyslawa Ziomkowa. So, he pursued his
studies as though his life depended on it. Tadeusz read
anything he could get his hands on. This passion made
him a well-read, knowledgeable young man who could
talk easily about any subject.

There was one book in particular that captured his
interest. It was called the *Sibylia* and was a complex book
of knowledge—historical, scientific, and spiritual. This
ancient book had somehow been translated into Polish
by some long forgotten scholar. The word *sibylia* was Latin
for oracle. In this text, this oracle was, most likely, the

prophetess Sibyl of Cumae, who offered one of her books to Tarquinius Superbus (a later king of Rome). There was a legend attached to this exchange between the two.

There were nine books of prophecy, regarding Rome's destiny, for which Sibyl demanded half the king's fortune. When he answered that the price was too high, she burned three books and offered him the other six at the same price. Still he hesitated, so she burned three more and he paid the original price for the remaining three. These Sibylline books were placed in the Temple of Jupiter on the Capitoline Hill and were consulted in times of emergency.

Also, in another Judeo-Christian legend, a prophetess was credited with the Sibylline Oracles. These were a collection of writings dating from 150 BC to 180 AD. However, we aren't sure whether the Polish version that Tadeusz owned originated from translations of the remaining three books of prophecy, or merely from portions of the Sibylline Oracles (along with other works).

If this was the same book that the legends spoke of, it was quite a wonderful book. It contained descriptions of a crystal that ancient Egyptians used to communicate over long distances and of wars that were to be fought in future years. It told of the "yellow race" that would populate the earth in such numbers that they would become a threat to the earth. (The Chinese, who have been derogatorily referred to as "yellow," realized their overpopulation in the 1970s). There would be wars fought with people of the "yellow race." This could be applied to Vietnam, and perhaps to another future war, since it spoke of world involvement.

The text also described biological experiments, the essence of life and how it originated, the curing of various diseases, and how to work with plants to achieve cures. One experiment explained how to get trees to bear several different types of fruits. Tadeusz tried this experiment and grafted seven different varieties of apples and pears onto the same tree. The tree actually bore fruit of a different variety on each branch. He also tried an experiment in which he mixed a solution of different chemicals that he rubbed onto the surface of a crystal glass. The glass began to give off sounds and humming vibrations as if by magic.

The book was filled with knowledge, some of which was not so acceptable to the general public. It talked about black magic, Satanism, spells, and curses. It also contained descriptions of white magic spells. It was all of this magic that Tadeusz's mother (Antonina) objected to. She was a religious woman and anything that was objectionable to the Catholic Church was not allowed in her household. She put an end to her son's studies by grabbing the book from him, as he was reading by the fireplace, and then flinging it into the fire. It met a fate similar to the books of Tarquinius Superbus. Tadeusz was disappointed that he had never finished reading the book and that he hadn't memorized more information from it. However, many years later, Tadeusz met a few other fortunate individuals who had also read the Sybilline book. Although we know the book is still around, he was unable to acquire the rare tome again.

⇒ 8 ⇐

1928–1935
Helena's Developing Psychic Abilities

By the age of nine, Helena displayed a number of psychic abilities. She found her abilities amusing and used them to entertain herself and her friends. "Table tapping" was the first unusual ability that she developed. In order to do this, she would sit at her heavy, oak kitchen table and touch her fingertips to the edge. Her fingertips would just rest lightly on the table and then she would ask a question. If the answer to her question was yes, the table would rise up on two legs and dropped down once. For no, it would rise up and drop down twice making thudding noises. Helena, her sister Stasia, and later on her cousin, Antosia, were all able to do table tapping, so she didn't think it was so unique. As far as she knew, everybody had the same abilities she had. The children would ask silly questions, such as whether they were having chicken for supper or whether a friend was coming over that evening. The answers were quite accurate, which thoroughly puzzled everyone. Her parents felt uneasy watching the table rise off the floor onto two legs. It wasn't as if Helena was physically picking up the side of the table. That would have been impossible since the only contact she had with the table was the tips of her fingers, and yet, there was the table, moving up and down!

Soon thereafter, Helena developed the skill of automatic handwriting. While she was holding a pencil loosely upon a piece of paper, or a piece of chalk on a slate, she could ask a question and get a written answer to her questions. This ability began one day as she was aimlessly doodling on her writing slate. Her hand began to write out sentences. It gave her information of all kinds, as well as incomprehensible scribbles. As to the source of this information, she had a number of theories. Helena felt that it was a dead relative who was supplying her with the information. Over the years, other people have suggested that the sources of automatic handwriting can originate from the subconscious mind, the universal consciousness of mankind, or by communicating with spirit entities.

There was one incident, however, that gave Helena's family respect for her unusual abilities. Her cousin Antonina Kot (they called her Antosia) had suffered from epilepsy since she was four. The first epileptic fit appeared to have been brought on by a neighbor. Antosia had accidentally fallen asleep while tending the family livestock and the cows wandered away and began eating the neighbor's grain. The neighbor became furious and took a stick and started to beat Antosia as she slept. She woke up with a start and immediately went into convulsions. The epileptic seizures continued through the next few years, and her parents tried every medicine and therapy available at that time. Antosia's parents spent thousands of zloty (dollars) on shots and medical treatments. Nothing worked and her epileptic fits began getting worse. Her parents were sure she would die since the doctors said they couldn't cure her. At a loss for anything else to do, Antosia's mother finally tried a remedy that Helena had received from one of her automatic handwriting sessions. She felt that her daughter had nothing to lose. According to Helena's instructions, they wrapped Antosia in steaming sheets, which had been soaked in a heavy sea salt solution. Then they covered her up with quilts and had her drink a tea brewed from the boiled bark and needles of the eastern larch tree (Modrzew). The tea from this tree was also ingested with all her meals. After less than three months of this treatment, the epileptic fits ceased and never returned.

After this successful treatment, the three children (Stasia, Antosia, and Helena) were allowed to "dabble in the unknown." No one in the family put any restrictions on them, but no one talked about it publicly either. It had been Antosia's cure that had allowed them to put aside all the old skepticism regarding Helena's abilities. However, there were still no good explanations as to what exactly was happening.

According to Edgar Cayce (1877–1945), America's most documented psychic of all times, anyone could develop the ability to do automatic handwriting. Cayce himself was able to provide information while in a state of trance. He provided a multitude of medical information, and other instructions, which cured a number of people. All of this was authenticated, and all his readings are kept on file at the Edgar Cayce Foundation in Virginia Beach, Virginia. On the subject of automatic handwriting, Cayce warned people to be careful of the source of the messages. In order to get a good source, or a good message, a person's intentions must be good. According to Cayce, a person should look within themselves for answers while asking to commune with the cosmic forces, or God. So long as the individual pursued the development of their psychic abilities for the benefit of others, not for materialistic gain, and in a noble, constructive, spiritual manner, they would be rewarded with success. Psychic abilities are gifts from God and should not be used for selfish or trivial reasons.[1]

Over the years, various explanations for Helena's psychic abilities were proposed. Perhaps the various accidents that Helena had lived through could have stimulated her psychic perception and ability. Similarly, her cousin Antosia, who also eventually displayed some ability to do table tapping, could have gained that ability because of the trauma and illness she had undergone—trauma and life threatening ailments are often noted as being linked to a heightened psychic awareness. Both of these cousins developed their abilities soon after their individual traumas. However, it is also possible that their psychic abilities were inherited. This certainly makes looking at the family tree much more interesting, especially if you can trace some of your ancestors' abilities to yourself.[2] The author of The ESP Enigma, Diane Hennacy Powell, stated in an article that genetics are likely behind psychic ability since it runs in families. There are also cases in which people haven't any psychic ability until they've suffered head traumas.

---

1 More information on Edgar Cayce's readings and psychic documents can be found at the Association for Research and Enlightenment, in Virginia Beach, VA or by accessing are-cayce.org/ecreadings. See reading 5752-2 on psychic development.

2 Stephey, M.J. ("The Science Behind Psychic Phenomena," Time Science Magazine, Dec. 24, 2008.) Accessed online at time.com.

Helena's abilities were developing and for the most part, she was using them to benefit others. However, children are children, and sometimes they treat their gifts like toys to be played with. Any number of difficult situations can arise when a psychic's ability is misused. Helena's family could not keep their daughter's psychic abilities hidden from the rest of the village for very long, especially since she decided to display her gift in front of strangers.

It was now 1931, and Helena was 13, and like other teenagers, she was eager to impress young males with her uniqueness. On one occasion, the parish priest was called in by some of the villagers to investigate the source of the children's powers. The girls had just scared the stuffing out of some local teenage boys, and their parents wanted to know what was going on. Apparently, the boys had decided to visit Helena's house because they had heard of the girls' ability to answer questions about the future. Helena and Stasia began their table tapping session and when the boys saw the table moving up and down, they were dumb-founded. They accused the girls of picking up the table with their fingertips, or of using trickery. After inspecting the heavy oak table, they found it impossible to move by just touching their fingertips to its edge. It was difficult to lift even using their arms. They could not duplicate the tapping movement.

Helena tried to explain to them what she felt like when she made the table move. She said the sensation would begin at the tips of her fingers, as though her fingers were sticky with a sort of magnetism. Then she would feel a tingling sensation going up her arms, to her spine, and then up through her neck into the base of her brain. It would feel as though the table were physically connected to her body. Of course, the boys didn't believe what she was saying. Soon the three boys got silly and sat down on top of the table. One of them said, "Okay, now answer this question." They asked their question. The table began straining, creaking, and soon lifted itself up onto two legs. Then the table began bouncing up and down as if to dislodge them. The boys freaked out. They ran out of the house screaming.

That same day, the Catholic priest from the village arrived. He wanted to be sure that no demonic powers were at work in his parish. He observed them, asked them religious questions, and finally determined that, whatever this power was, it wasn't based on anything evil. However, he encouraged them not to pursue this unusual ability and not to allow evil to influence idle minds. He told them that spirits often try to communicate with the living but they should not be kept tied down to this mortal plane by playing inconsequential games with them. Furthermore, the good spirits could possibly be exposed to attacks or detention by evil spirits. Then the priest told them not to play this "game" any more. He blessed the house and the children, and he left. Actually, as far as Catholic priests of that era went, this priest was fairly open-minded. However, just like many other religious individuals, he labeled psychic abilities as unsafe and unnatural. He discouraged the development of the children's psychic abilities. Fortunately, his admonitions did not stifle Helena's abilities.

Helena displayed a particular gift in the form of dreaming about future events. Most of her dreams concerned simple things, such as visits from friends or events in school. However, there were often notable dreams, some with global significance.

Several years before the outbreak of World War II, Helena dreamed that she saw a large, fruitful field. Its crops were rich and hearty but were completely covered by black crows that were ravenously pecking at the field. Somehow she knew this scene meant that war was coming to Poland. Then, in a subsequent dream, Hitler (whose name was becoming more frequently mentioned in political discussions) came driving up to her house in a carriage. He drove so quickly that he drove through a flimsy wooden wall without even looking back. In the dream, Hitler saw Helena and told her that he was taking her away with him, out of Poland. Years later, this was exactly how Hitler drove through Poland during the start of WWII on September 1, 1939. He shattered Polish defenses, like a flimsy wall, and overran most of Western and Central Poland in two weeks.

Coming of Age in Biala Podlaska

Growing up is difficult enough for an ordinary child with the usual social pressures and the typical childhood dreams; however, Helena's life was particularly difficult without a father around the house. She missed him deeply. He was a good man, but his travels kept him away (he would either be on the other side of the world, or away on business), especially when she needed him most. People were often rude to her and abused her because they knew there was no man in the house to defend the family.

One disturbing incident occurred in school when Helena was about 12. She was sitting in front of another girl, named Josephine, who decided to pull Helena's long braids. Surprised by the sharp tug, she turned around to look at her tormentor. The teacher (Jan Kuczynski) was in the middle of a lecture when he saw her turn around. Using a ruler, he struck Helena's hand for not keeping her eyes up front. He hit her with such force that her hand swelled up to the size of an apple. However, he only scolded Josephine. Kuczynski would never have taken such brutal measures with Helena if he knew that her father was at home. If Wladyslaw had been home, he would have marched into the schoolhouse and confronted the brute (as other fathers had). But, throughout her childhood, there was never anyone Helena could depend on to keep her safe.

Even though Helena's childhood was not especially pleasant, you could never tell she was sad by her demeanor. She would constantly sing, hum, and whistle like a bird. People would know that Helena was coming long before they could see her. She had often heard that whatever you do best in life, you should offer that up to God. She decided to offer up her singing to Him as a gift . . . there was very little else she could offer in her humble life. She sang constantly in the church choir and was asked to be the soloist at all the important church festivities. This outlet for her talent, and her deeply held religious convictions, gave her a sense of identity and belonging. Religion became an important factor in her life. Helena had never received a lot of loving attention from her parents, so she never had a sense of her own self worth. She considered herself a plain, unattractive, ordinary child. The reality was that she was quite attractive, talented, and definitely out of the ordinary.

Sometimes, there were occasional moments of joy . . . like the summer when she was 13. Helena went to a week-long regional religious retreat. This church-sponsored outing was held several miles away from home and was attended by all the local youth groups. Various districts were represented by the attending youths. There were the usual church services and lectures, as well as the more enjoyable plays, music, singing, and dancing. Helena was looking forward to socializing with the other children, for it would help break up the monotony and drudgery of her life. Her world was one of constant hard work and responsibilities, so this outing was a much-anticipated release for her. Of course, she didn't expect to dance much, nor did she expect to be more than just a spectator at all the festivities. She knew she couldn't compete with her sister Stasia, who was quite popular. The boys were constantly flocking around Stasia whenever there was a dance. With her large bust and flirtatious manner, Stasia seldom sat out a dance alone. Helena, on the other hand, was much more reserved and serious-minded and preferred not to draw attention to herself. That summer however, everything changed for her.

The church retreat ended with a dance for all the participants. The band was playing lively, popular tunes, while the young people shyly paired up on the dance floor. Helena was sitting in the second row, tapping her foot in time to the music, when the most handsome young man she had ever seen in her life began walking in her direction. All the girls around her began to preen, wondering which one of them would be asked, but he looked past all of them and asked Helena if she would do him the honor of this dance. She was so shocked that for a moment she just sat there with her mouth wide open. Then, collecting her wits, she literally leaped over the front bench. She presented herself, without a scrap of sophistication, before him. He acted graciously, ignoring her flushed, embarrassed state. He danced beautifully. Their small talk consisted of "What's your name," and "Will you be here later after the dance?" Then he escorted her back to her seat, bowed over her hand, and kissed it.

She suddenly felt grown up, important, and pretty! He walked away from their area and talked with some of his classmates for a while. Helena could see that the other girls in her group were envious of her. She felt ecstatic. For the first time in her life, someone could be envious of her. Shortly thereafter, the handsome stranger returned, smiled at her, and asked her to dance again. This time she walked around the benches with a little more reserve and danced with him as though she danced with gorgeous young men every day of her life. He said he hoped she would be able to join him for supper that evening. She was dancing on air. Now she knew what Cinderella felt like when she was with her Prince Charming.

That afternoon, Helena's youth group left early in order to get home before dark. While others were still dancing at the outing, Helena left like Cinderella leaving the ball. It was a bittersweet ending to Helena's day. She wanted to spend the rest of the week dancing with her Prince, if only she could. But she knew she'd never see him again. When they arrived home, she excitedly told her father about the wonderful day she had just had. She danced through her chores, singing at the top of her voice, as the cows watched her in bewilderment.

Late that evening, she was sitting on the verandah with her family when some of the local young men stopped by the house. They called for Stasia to come join them at the church hall dance. Then one of them shouted out to Helena.

"Hey, we saw you dancing up a storm at the retreat. The other girls are jealous that you were the only one dancing from their group. Where did you learn to dance so well and how come you haven't been dancing with us? Are you too good for us, or something? We saw that dandy from the city you were dancing with. Is he your beau?"

They insisted that she go with them to the dance after showering her with more comments and jests. Her sister, Stasia, was giving her dirty looks for being the center of attention. Her mom said she was too young to go out with that crowd. However, her father had seen how much it meant to Helena, so he told his wife to let her go and have some fun. After all, she had an older sister who could chaperone and she'd have time to stay at home when she got older.

It might have been because of his own adventurous nature that he urged her to go out. But, whatever his reasons, Helena was overjoyed and grateful that he let her go. No longer would she have to practice dancing in a corner with a broom, or a younger cousin. She was old enough to dance with the adults.

❧ 9 ❧

1936
The Prophecy of Symbolerus
(Hermanta)

In 1936, Tadeusz Szelazek was 27 years old and the manager of a store (a franchise) called Spolem in Zabinka near Kobrin, in the district of Brzesc (Brest). The store was closed to celebrate a church holy day and he and some of the clerks from the store decided to go to a séance/lecture by Symbolerus. They called Symbolerus the hierophant (hermit) and although he was somewhat of a recluse, he would occasionally give demonstrations of his psychic abilities, as well as his skills with hypnotism.

During the psychic's lecture, one of the clerks was acting in an obnoxious, disrespectful manner. The noisy distraction he was causing caught the psychic's attention. He ordered the clerk to come forward and participate in a demonstration showing the powers of hypnosis. Although the young man resisted coming forward and held tightly onto his chair, a force seemed to drag him up and deposit him in front of Symbolerus. Apparently, the clerk was an easy subject to hypnotize.

This noisy young man had a variety of faults, including a nasty personality. Very often he would ridicule others for their clothes, their beliefs, and so on. He thought nothing of hurting people's feelings. It was very interesting to watch Symbolerus convince him to strip to his underwear, telling him that it was his bedtime. The clerk got on the couch and was preparing for sleep when Symbolerus brought him out of the hypnotic state—to the clerk's great embarrassment. This humiliating experience, and the exposure to ridicule, made an impression on him. It took a long time before he could face anyone. His usually nasty attitude disappeared, and he no longer made fun of people just for the sport of it.

After the hypnosis demonstration, the crowd began dispersing. Tadeusz introduced himself to Symbolerus and started a conversation with him about the paranormal. When Symbolerus asked him about his background, Tadeusz told him (in his usual joking fashion) that he was born an orphan, never had a mother, and never knew his father. He wasn't going to give the man any clues to his background since he had always been skeptical of psychics. So, he was taken completely off guard when the man told him all about his family. Not only did he tell him that both his parents were alive, but also the present state of their health. Then Symbolerus proceeded to give Tadeusz an outline of his future.

"You will marry a woman named Helena. She has dark blond hair and blue eyes. She will appear to have good financial prospects, and a good dowry, but you will not get one zloty (dollar) from this marriage. Instead, you will invest your own money into this union and not profit by it."

"What? Never? Why would I go along with such an arrangement?"

"Such is your fate. But there is more . . . . You will leave the country of your birth—Poland. You will live and die in a foreign country."

"Why would I want to leave Poland? My family is here. We've lived here for centuries. My job is here. My future is here, where my past has been."

"It won't be up to you whether you live here or not. There will be a Great War, which will involve the whole world, and these circumstances will dictate your choices. You will be on the front lines of the war, but you will go through the cataclysm physically unscathed. You will go through a hail of bullets but none will touch you. Your enemies will be plentiful throughout your life, like mushrooms after the rain. But, like mushrooms, you can step on them and crush them into insignificance. How-ever, you will bestow the ultimate humiliation to your enemies by helping them in their time of need and show-ing them mercy."

"Why would I show mercy or help an enemy? Shouldn't we want to see our enemies dead or at least humiliated?"

"It's not so simple. Everyone has a purpose in life and each person affects everybody else's purpose in life. We are all a part of a scheme of existence that we cannot comprehend with our limited minds. God can avenge the harm done to you in a manner that you cannot even imagine; perhaps even more harshly than you would have chosen. If you deal justly with others, treating them as you would want to be treated; you will be supported by God throughout your life."

"You said I was to be married. Will I have children?"

"You will have six children . . . three sons and three daughters. Your sons will all die. This will be a great sor-row to you, but this too is beyond your control."

"What about wealth?"

"Wealth means different things to different people. You can be wealthy if you so desire, however, you may choose not to be. That will be your choice when the opportunity presents itself. You will be well off, comfortable, and happy before you die, and that will be at the age of 72."

At this point Tadeusz became agitated. He had listened to tales of war, death of children, leaving his homeland, giving away his money, and his responsibilities to God and man. Such a gloomy psychic reading didn't leave much to be overjoyed about. He reacted with anger.

"How can you presume to tell me how old I will be when I die, or even if I'm ever going to die?"

Symbolerus seemed to hesitate and then stared at him for a moment.

"You're absolutely correct. I am only telling you what I see. But, your future is between you and God. If you find, at the appointed time, that there is something you have to accomplish, something that will be of service to God and man, your time will be extended. That will be between God and you. The length of your life is part of the contract you established with God before you were ever born. But remember one thing; keep God in your life. He is found everywhere. He dwells in every church, synagogue, mosque, palace, shack, or mountain top."

So, in this manner, the conversation that predicted the life of Tadeusz Szelazek ended. At the time, Tadeusz did not think the reading was of any special importance. He was not accustomed to putting credence into the words of "prophets." The evening had been entertaining, but he felt that the future was not predicted in backwater towns of Poland.

Part II

The Approaching Exile
and Fulfilling Fate

☞ 10 ☜

Meeting and Marrying Helena

You will marry a woman named Helena. She has blond hair and
blue eyes . . .

After managing the Spolem franchise and training
in Wloclawki, Tadeusz moved to Kobrin near Brzesc (Brest). Eventually, he became the store manager in
Zabinka (near Kobrin), and worked there for two years.
During this time he was able to save enough money to
purchase his own franchise store in Dywin. It was in
Dywin that his life began to unfold, as was foretold.

One Sunday, Tadeusz attended services in a village
church in Dywin. During the service, he heard an angelic
voice coming from the choir loft. The woman's beautiful soprano voice immediately captivated Tadeusz. He
attended as many masses as he possibly could, until he
finally got an opportunity to meet her. The soloist's name
was Helena Semerylo and he fell in love with her almost
immediately. She had blue eyes, dark blond hair, and a
gentle, sympathetic nature that sometimes hid her actual
strength, courage, and perseverance. Tadeusz sensed
honor and loyalty in her. He had been searching for these
qualities in a woman all his life. Now, at the age of 28, he
had finally found someone special.

Helena Semerylo, however, was unaware of the esteem Tadeusz held for her. She merely saw herself as independent and hardworking. She had been only 16 when she moved to Dywin to stay with her Aunt Bronislawa and her Uncle Wladyslaw Brodacki. The couple was childless and needed help running their estate. Her uncle had received land from the Polish government for his services in the military during WWI. He tried for some time to make his estate fruitful and profitable but had not succeeded. His wife had had several children (Helena had even assisted at two of the births); however, none had lived past the age of two. Helena's aunt and uncle needed her help since they could not afford (or trust) hired hands to work the land. So, Helena left her home in Korczowka to work for them.

In a way, the move provided her with a future since Helena's sister, Stasia, was destined to inherit their parents' land. Stasia was newly married to a man named Wiktor Filipiuk and had refused to give up any portion of the family estate as a dowry for Helena. By rights, Helena was entitled to some money upon her engagement and she could have fought to get it, but she never considered suing them because it would have created unpleasantness for her parents. Instead, Helena gave up her claim to a dowry. Her aunt's estate, which she thought she was to inherit, fulfilled the role of a dowry, and seemed a promising start for a future marriage. Helena felt the hope and security that owning land could provide.

It was at this juncture in Helena's life that Tadeusz moved into the little village of Dywin. Tadeusz enjoyed his life in these new surrounds where he often shared his time and expertise in local community services. He became involved with church youth groups, instructing them in theater, acting, and other activities. He was quite talented; in fact, he was one of the best amateur actors in the district. People came from miles around to see him act and to see the plays he directed. With all the attention he was generating, he quickly became noticed by the ladies in the area. He also came to the attention of the parish priest in Dywin; a man named Father Tomkiewicz.

Father Tomkiewicz had a rich, spinster friend for whom he wanted to arrange a marriage. This lady was 38, rather fat, and unattractive. However, she had money, some of which the priest hoped would be donated to his collection box. He actually promised the spinster that Tadeusz would marry her. Nevertheless, in spite of all the priest's efforts to try to convince him to be a suitor, Tadeusz was determined to marry Helena.

Father Tomkiewicz had to devise a plan to break up the budding romance if he was going to accomplish his long-range profitable scheme. He decided that the only way he could get the pair to break up was to slander one party to the other. Tomkiewicz told Tadeusz that Helena was just an ordinary, ignorant peasant. He proceeded to tell another vile, slanderous, and shocking lie: It was well known, he claimed, that she was ill with venereal disease. The priest knew she was a good, innocent, hard-working girl with a good reputation. After all, he had heard everyone's confessions (the entire village confessed to him) and knew what type of person Helena was. However, Tomkiewicz was in a perfect position to manipulate anyone he chose. Who wouldn't believe a priest? Fortunately Tadeusz realized what the priest was up to.

When the lies failed to dissuade Tadeusz, Tomkiewicz turned his attentions to Helena. The priest told her that the store Tadeusz owned was bankrupt because he was embezzling. His creditors were hounding him, and he was a dishonest man without honor. This greatly surprised

Helena. She asked Tomkiewicz why a scoundrel like that would be allowed to lead youth groups sponsored by the church. Why were Szelazek's shelves stocked with fresh goods and his store filled with customers? She was in a quandary. Certainly the priest was wrong.

Helena tried to get to the bottom of all the rumors. It was difficult to get satisfactory answers. Tadeusz always had a habit of speaking well of everyone. So when Helena asked if the priest was a good man, Tadeusz had answered, "yes." That answer didn't help her understand what was going on. She didn't want to repeat the slanders she had heard, so she finally decided to confront the priest in the confessional. Helena asked him if he would swear an oath that Tadeusz was as disreputable as he claimed. She had caught him at his game. This infuriated Tomkiewicz who started screaming at her, calling her names and finally storming out of the confessional. He knew he had failed. Now he would have to tell the spinster that the suitor got away.

Shortly after Christmas, Tadeusz and Helena were engaged. The Catholic Church required that the couple be questioned by a priest who would assess their knowledge of catechism and the responsibilities of marriage. Only a satisfactory review would allow them to be married. Naturally, as the parish priest, it was up to Tomkiewicz to ask the questions and review their catechism. Given their previous history, the couple knew he would make things as difficult as possible for them. But Tadeusz was ready for him.

Father Tomkiewicz began the review. He asked them what "penitence and sorrow for sins" meant. Tadeusz began to explain the meaning of penitence, the reasoning involved in how one became aware of what a sin was.

"No!" screamed the priest, "I want the answer in verse form, exactly the way it's written in the catechism book."

"Okay," said Tadeusz, "If you want verse, then I will give you verse . . . . Penitence for sins means you should grit your teeth, beat your head on the wall, and your ass on the ground! I'm through playing your games! You, as a *servant* of God, the church, and man, will do as you are told! You will marry us on February second and you will post the wedding banns accordingly!"

Tadeusz and Helena chose their wedding day (February 2, 1939) to coincide with a church holy day called Matki Boskej Gromnicznej (Candlemas). Father Tomkiewicz was still angry with the young couple for outwitting him and for forcing him to marry them. He thought that he would punish the upstart couple by not wearing ceremonial vestments for the mass. The whole congregation observed this obvious insult because it was customary for the priest to be dressed in his best vestments for major holy day celebrations. Candlemas celebrated the purification of the Virgin Mary and the presentation of the infant Jesus in the Temple. It was an important holy day for the Catholic people in Dywin. On this holy day, people brought in candles, which were blessed for use in religious ceremonies in their homes.

Tomkiewicz ordered the staff to keep the church in darkness—no electric lights, or candles, were lit. This was his attempt to do whatever he could to ruin the ceremony for Tadeusz and Helena. The church organist, however, quickly organized the choir to sing for this special couple against the priest's express wishes. After all, the organist respected Helena immensely. Her magnificent voice had been heard at every Sunday mass and holy day for years.

He also admired her goodness and generosity. So, for him, it was easy to defy the orders.

The church was packed that day, although few people in the congregation were aware of the wedding that was to be held. The church was not decorated, nor were there flowers on the altar; nothing indicated that a wedding was in progress. Tomkiewicz had seen to that. However, the congregation had brought flowers, as they usually did for holy days, and their scent filled the building. Then, because it was dark inside the church, everyone lit the candles that they had brought with them to be blessed that day. The ceremony turned out to be more beautiful then the couple could have planned.

⁓ 11 ⁓

A Stolen Visit Home

She will appear to have good financial prospects and a good dowry but you will not get one zloty from this marriage.

Tadeusz spent a lot of his own money to properly attire Helena and himself for the wedding. Helena had no dowry, and no finances of her own, with which to buy clothes. Stasia and her husband had taken over her parents' home, refusing to give Helena a penny from the estate. Her father was willing to sell a fourth of the land to give Helena a dowry, but Stasia and her mother voted him down. Stasia had convinced everyone that since she decided to remain on the estate with her husband, she would be the one responsible for her parents' welfare. She felt she had to hold onto the entire estate and all the finances. Helena was on her own, especially since she was already "farmed-out" to the Brodackis. She was the Brodackis' responsibility now.

Tadeusz borrowed 200 zloty from his brother Stanislaw to pay for the clothes and wedding arrangements. Stach, as his brother was called, took full advantage of the situation by making himself at home in the little store. He began taking produce from the shelves, and change from the cash register, whenever he felt like it. In effect, he made himself a partner in the business and Tadeusz couldn't get Stach out of the store without repaying the loan. All Tadeusz's money was tied up in inventory and times were unstable. Once Stach got inside, he made a great nuisance of himself in every way imaginable. When Tadeusz finally had the money to repay the loan, Stach refused to accept it saying he was a partner and would not be bought out.

Tadeusz had hoped that, after the marriage to Helena, he could sell the store and build a house on the Brodacki estate. Selling the store would dissolve the "partnership" with Stach and give him a tidy nest egg with which to begin another venture. However, the situation at the Brodacki farm was not what it appeared to be. Helena's uncle and aunt had assured her that she would eventually inherit the land. Believing that to be so, Tadeusz bought a plow horse for the farm, made repairs to the build-ings, harvested crops, and invested his own money into the property. Unfortunately, he was unaware of Helena's uncle's and aunt's true natures. They were stingy, lazy, and uncharitable toward everyone, particularly their niece. Wladyslaw and Bronislawa Brodacki treated Helena as their own personal Cinderella. She cleaned, cooked, ran errands, tended the farm animals, harvested the crops, and did everything for free. They saw her more as an indentured servant than as a family member. It was highly doubtful that they intended to give Helena anything, other than work.

As a result of their situation, Tadeusz and Helena had no time for a honeymoon. They couldn't have afforded one anyhow, but they had hoped to get away for a few days when the weather turned warmer. Opportunities to relax were few and far between and they looked forward to some kind of break in the unrelenting work.

A dance was being held in the village two weeks after their wedding. The young couple decided to attend, although even that brief respite presented a problem for them. Uncle Brodacki protested loudly. He insisted that they couldn't go dancing with all the work that needed to be done. When they went anyway, he began cursing them out as if they were his children and they had disobeyed his orders. He begrudged the newly married couple even a few hours of fun and relaxation. They left for the dance, but the mood was spoiled.

A month later (March 1939), Aunt Bronislawa decided to go visit relatives in another part of Poland. Helena took over all her aunt's responsibilities, plus her own, which meant running the whole estate. Uncle Brodacki was always too cheap to hire outside help, so the following days became exhausting. Things became especially difficult when the cattle contracted hoof and mouth disease. Helena spent hours tending the animals and trying to stop the progress of the disease. She worked so hard that she physically weakened herself and kept getting nosebleeds. She had had recurring problems with severe headaches and pain ever since her childhood accident; however, over the years she learned not to complain. There was usually no one to complain to.

The one time she did complain would always remain in her memory. Helena was only 14 at the time when she complained to her mother about the intense pain in her head. They were working in the fields where she was digging potatoes. She had to bag them and then lug the 50 pound bags to the wagon. When she complained, her mother told her, "My head hurts even more than yours does." Well, if that was true, Helena felt she should not complain. She didn't say another word; instead she passed out from the pain. It was only then that her mother realized that her child was not just whining. From then on, Helena tried to bear pain stoically, but it seemed her fate in life that people would always downplay her suffering.

Time passed, and still her aunt did not return from her trip. April turned to May and then May turned into June. By now Helena knew she was pregnant. She was excited about starting a family; nothing could give her greater happiness. It was just difficult to feel happy with all the responsibility that was placed upon her. Morning sickness and hard work were taking their toll on her. Aunt Bronislawa wrote a letter in June, saying she probably wouldn't be back in July, but maybe the following month. After all, the chores were left in the capable hands of her niece, so she didn't see the need to return quickly.

Tadeusz had had enough of the Brodackis' neglect of the farm. He was also disgusted with the unfair advantages they were taking of their niece. By taking advantage of her, they were also taking advantage of him. Tadeusz had been dividing his time between running the store and helping out on the Brodacki estate. He needed a vacation desperately and he needed time to be with his new bride. Tadeusz had told the Brodackis that he had intended to visit Helena's parents during the summer. Neither one of them had seen their friends or relatives since before the wedding. Now it was already August and Aunt Bronislawa was not at home to relieve Helena of her duties. It was obvious that the Brodackis were ignoring his wishes.

So, he decided enough was enough! They packed a few clothes, got on their bikes and began the ride from Dywin to Korczowka. It was a long trip by bike (approximately 134 km), but it was one that Helena had done frequently since she was 14. Bus tickets would have been too expensive for the couple, so they had no other option than to ride their bikes.

It was during the drive toward her old home that Helena had an accident. The brakes on her bike failed as they were speeding down a hill. She couldn't slow herself down fast enough as she tried pulling out of a curve. The resulting crash, into a tree, left her jarred and frightened. She had fallen, and although there wasn't a lot of physical damage, she started to worry about injury to the baby she was carrying. They rested for a while, and then they stopped at a restaurant on the way. This was the first time Helena had ever eaten in a restaurant and she loved the experience. However, even that pleasant experience was marred by her worries about her unborn baby's safety.

They stayed for nearly a week at Helena's parents' house. Her sister Stasia was as unsympathetic and ungracious as usual. She told Helena not to look for any money or possessions at "her" house. She was the eldest and everything there was hers. Helena should be grateful to the Brodackis for being "so kind to her." Helena was hurt and upset that her family never understood what her life was like with the Brodackis. She was being taken advantage of and abused by her aunt and uncle, but no one seemed to care or understand.

Although it had been Helena's intention to visit her family and enjoy a warm reunion, the constant reminder of her inferior position in the family, and her lack of money, hurt her deeply. So, after listening to her sister's comments, Helena wished her sister a similar fate. She told her, "May you also experience the sort of kindness I have been receiving for the rest of your life."

During that week at her parents' they happened to bump into Aunt Brodacka who had been "vacationing" now for six months. When she saw them there, she panicked. "Who's tending the farm?" Tadeusz answered her, "definitely not you!" She took off the next day, back to her husband and the farm.

Tadeusz and Helena spent a couple of days more visiting with her parents and some of her friends. When it was time to leave, her father Wladyslaw escorted them to the edge of town. He reached into his pocket and brought out some change.

"I don't have much to give you. You deserve a dowry and much more, but I'm not in a position to give it to you. Your mother and sister do not agree with me on this matter. They say they have no intentions of being reduced to poverty by sharing with you at this time. All I can give you is my love and my blessing. It is all I have and I hope that will be enough for now."

Helena gave her father a heartfelt kiss. It would be a long time before she saw him again. The tears she shed as she left him were not just from parting; she was crying from all the injustice she seemed to be constantly encountering throughout her life.

⮞ 12 ⮜

Poland Is Invaded

You will bestow the ultimate humiliation upon your enemies by helping them in their time of need and showing them mercy.

Poland was now entering a period of political distress. Many informed citizens knew that Hitler was planning an invasion, but most didn't want to believe it. Surely, if all the countries in the League of Nations were to stand up to the Germans, an invasion couldn't happen. Some Polish people naively believed that other nations would never allow one to take place. They even felt that the Russians, who were historically anti-German, would come to their aid. Despite Hitler's obviously aggressive tactics in Europe, the French and English governments actually advised Poland not to reveal any armament build-up so they wouldn't upset Germany. The atmosphere of German "appeasement" was not conducive to preparing a country for war. On April 28, 1939, Hitler renounced the German-Polish nonaggression treaty. It was obvious what would happen next.

Hitler finally invaded Poland on September 1, 1939. The British and French declared war on Germany, but it was too late for Poland. Despite the declaration of war, no one came to the aid of the Poles. International treaties, pacts, agreements, and friendships were all irrelevant. Poland was doomed. Their freedom and identity as a nation was over.

In eastern Poland, self-appointed Byelorussian vigilantes were "policing" the villages. They were called *kurokrady* (chicken-thieves) by the Polish citizens, because of their habit of stealing from the local landowners. Only a small percentage of Polish citizens lived in the eastern part of the country. The majority of the population was Russian, Ukrainian, Byelorussian, and so on. Even though they were in the minority, the Poles who lived there were considered the elite of the local society. These citizens included teachers, shopkeepers, clergy, and major landowners. The landowners acquired the land in WWI as a reward for their efforts. The land itself had changed hands innumerable times between the Russians and Poles. Centuries of dual ownership clouded boundary lines and kept disputes fresh in the minds of the people. Some of the Byelorussians in the area saw this new disturbance as an occasion to turn the tide of political power. They were also hopeful that some land might, in turn, be handed over to them. The vigilantes, however, disregarded everyone's best interests except their own. Their goals were to immediately attain money, property, and amusement at the expense of the Poles. They began harassing Polish soldiers, and other local volunteers, who were going to the western front. These soldiers often had only bikes as transportation. They were poor but determined to go west and defend Poland from the Germans. Often, the vigilantes would rob them of their bikes and possessions. In some cases, the volunteers were also beaten as well as robbed.

Tadeusz could not stand by and allow these thefts and harassment to continue. He called upon a number of local leaders to see if they could influence the vigilantes. He knew that most of what was going on was done with their approval, but he appealed to them anyway.

"Today you allow an attack upon a Polish soldier and stand by while they steal his bike. But, perhaps tomorrow, when the Germans attack our town, we'll need that soldier to protect us. It doesn't make sense to allow the harassment of someone who may be our salvation in the future."

Finally, an official order was sent out to stop the harassment of soldiers upon pain of imprisonment or death. It did help the situation to a certain extent. However, in general, the citizens of the surrounding area tended to ignore the raiders, so long as they didn't "police" too many of their chickens.

The Russians betrayed Poland and aided the Germans when they divided Poland on September 17, 1939. Poland was partitioned between Germany and Russia as the Supreme Soviet formally admitted Western Ukraine and Western Byelorussia into the USSR. Russian soldiers, and citizens, were capturing and killing Polish soldiers. The Germans came so close to Brzesc (Brest) that Tadeusz saw the flashes from bomb explosions in neighboring Kobrin.

Eventually, a large company of retreating Polish soldiers made its way back through their region. They were avoiding the Germans but continuing to regroup as much as possible. Despite the fact that the Russians were now the enemy as well, they continued to move east and south. As the Polish soldiers entered the town of Dywin, where Tadeusz had his store, the "policemen" (as the vigilantes called themselves) foolishly attacked the first ragtag group of soldiers. Unfortunately for them, the Byelorussian men hadn't realized just how large the company was when they began their assault. Four of the vigilantes were caught and the Polish commanding officer gave orders to have the town surrounded and set on fire. They would burn out all these traitors of Poland.

The town's pharmacist, Milorowicz, whose family was originally from Odessa, ran to beg the officer to spare the town.

"Please, Mr. Officer, don't punish the whole town for the actions of a few."

The pharmacist's words just aggravated the situation further. Nothing he said moved the officer until Tadeusz approached and addressed him. He immediately caught the officer's attention since he could correctly identify the officer's rank and insignia. He spoke to the colonel with a beautifully refined accent and a vocabulary that indicated a Polish education. Tadeusz needed him to understand that this town contained Polish people who were not German sympathizers.

"Colonel, sir, I beg you to consider that many important, loyal citizens of this town are Polish citizens like yourself. You will be burning us out along with these Russians. We have to remain living here among both the Germans and the Russians or cease to exist completely. You can burn down our town, but you will leave the rest of us at the disposal of our enemies when you leave. Let's not kill our own people for the sake of a few enemies."

The Colonel rescinded the order to burn the village but ordered the lieutenant to set up a firing squad on the outskirts of town to execute the four vigilantes. Tadeusz followed them up to the designated area accompanied by the pharmacist. The firing squad was getting set up for the execution when, again, Tadeusz pleaded to have the four lives spared.

"Today you still have the power of life or death over this small part of Poland, but things are changing. By sparing their lives, you would be sending a message of nobility, mercy, and understanding in the true Polish spirit. These enemies of today may become the friends of tomorrow. The Russian people of this village may look more favorably upon sparing our retreating soldiers now that the war is going badly for us. Perhaps they will even treat them with the nobility you showed today. You will have shown them a good example to follow."

The colonel considered this for a moment and then spat in disgust. He took a white pair of gloves out of his pocket and slapped the faces of the four people.

"This is your death today! You are less than men. You have no honor. Without honor, a man is dead. Remember this day well, the next time you try to attack another Polish soldier."

Then he turned to Tadeusz.

"You have argued their case strongly and justly. These are your prisoners. I leave them to you to deal with them as you see fit; although they really do deserve to die."

The company of soldiers left. The four pardoned men fell on their knees and tried to kiss Tadeusz's feet. He told them to get up and to show mercy to others in the future, even if they were enemies. This event had a profound affect on the population of the area. After this incident, Polish soldiers, who managed to pass through the district, were ignored or even aided in their retreat.

As fate would have it, among the four people who were saved was a man named Kloczkowicz. He would later play an important role in Tadeusz and Helena's life.

≈ 13 ≈

The Last Days in Poland

Everyone has a purpose in life and each person affects everybody else's purpose in life.

The Polish people still couldn't believe what was happening. They were stunned by this quickly evolving war. Polish soldiers who were trying to regroup were being attacked and captured by the Russians. Priests were being killed; Jews were being deported and murdered. The Poles were trying to hide and help escapees in whatever way they could—by feeding them, giving them shelter and safety, and so on—even though all the houses were being searched by German and Russian soldiers. It was total pandemonium. Some Polish soldiers and civilians fled toward Czechoslovakia. Some escaped, and some were captured.

When the war erupted, Tadeusz was ineligible for service and was classified in the "C" category so he had not joined the army. He was, and always remained, a small, thin, wiry man, who weighed no more than 135 pounds his entire life. He had been deemed "of a weak constitution" by the enlistment board. He was only to be called for active duty during times of war, at which time he would have been assigned a desk job. However, when the defense of Poland collapsed, which it did in a matter of days, there wasn't even an opportunity to volunteer. There wasn't any time, and there was no longer a Polish Army to volunteer for!

The Russian Communists seized and officially annexed Poland, installing their Russian Security Police (NKVD) in the local government offices. Many of the Byelorussian and Ukrainian citizens in the Kobrin/Brzesc districts served as officials for the Russian government. All guns and armaments were confiscated from the citizens. Anyone who failed to turn in a weapon (if a gun were discovered on their person or property) would be executed on the spot.

For the newly married couple, life on the Brodackis' estate was more miserable than ever. Coupled with the stress and destruction surrounding them, uncle Brodacki still treated the young couple like his personal slaves. He thought he had two indentured servants for the price of one.

Early one morning, Brodacki rushed into Tadeusz's bedroom, where he and Helena were still fast asleep. He was waving a pitchfork at them and shouting.

"Get up you slut, get up and work."

He moved the pitchfork as though to stab at them, so Tadeusz pulled out a handgun from under their pillow and aimed it at Brodacki's head. The uncle backed off saying Tadeusz would regret this later. Shortly thereafter, on December 23, 1939, the local police pulled Tadeusz and Helena in for questioning. And there, sitting at the station, was her aunt. The police chief, Kloczkowicz (one of the men whose life had been saved by Tadeusz) was interrogating her.

"You saw a gun?"

"Yes."

"Did you see the bullets?"

"No."

"Well, what good is a gun without bullets? Don't waste my time. You have no case. It's obvious you don't like your niece's husband, but that's not our concern."

"He does nothing for us whatsoever; he even brought a horse onto our farm just to eat up our grain."

"Yes, as though I would believe that you're not getting any work out of that horse, like you aren't getting any work out of your niece and her husband. Go home, woman!"

After she left, the chief let out a sigh of relief. He told Tadeusz and Helena that it was a good thing that the woman was stupid and that she hadn't insisted on pressing charges, because they were both in a serious predicament. If it hadn't been for his indebtedness to Tadeusz, he would have been required to arrest him and execute him by a firing squad. However, knowing how honorable and merciful Tadeusz had been with people—like himself—Kloczkowicz wasn't about to let a witch like Brodacka destroy him. He would later collect the handgun personally from Tadeusz so that there would be no weapons on the premises. Kloczkowicz didn't want the Brodackis to create more trouble for the young couple. Personally, he felt it was ridiculous that the aunt would have created a situation that would have deprived the family of a weapon—a weapon that they all needed for protection. Kloczkowicz was the law around here, but he could not single-handedly maintain peace during wartime. A weapon was absolutely vital during dangerous times like these.

"By the way, Szelazek, shouldn't you be starting a family soon instead of starting trouble?" he joked.

Little did he know that Helena was already eight months pregnant, but she was carrying it well. The winter coat she was wearing covered up her pregnancy.

Helena gave birth to their son Eugeniusz (Eugene) on January 6, 1940. He was a beautiful child with blond hair and blue eyes. He was the joy of their lives and made the tragic times they lived in more bearable. Geniusz, as they called him, even lessened the tension at the Brodacki estate somewhat—an almost impossible achievement!

Following the questioning at the police station, the Brodackis wisely left Tadeusz alone. They knew that he could not (and would not) easily forget their betrayal, however. If the Russian official had been anyone else but Kloczkowicz, Tadeusz would have been shot. Helena would have been a widow, in the middle of a war, with a tiny infant to take care of. The Brodackis were at a definite disadvantage. Not only were their true characters exposed, but they also exposed the whole family to danger. The handgun had been the only weapon in the house. They were all defenseless now. However, there were plenty of other worries to concern themselves with these days. There were rumors that all the Poles in this part of the country were to be removed from their homes.

In the beginning of February, Helena developed an abscess on one of her breasts. This is a fairly common occurrence for new nursing mothers, especially if they live in non-sterile environments. The farm was anything but sterile. Helena's pain intensified as the breast became more inflamed. So, on February 9, Helena went to the doctor at the local clinic, but he couldn't help her. He said she would have to come back the next day to get an injection. Disappointed, and hurting, she started the walk back to her home when a stranger with a Byelorussian accent stopped her.

"Lady, you don't know me, but I need to warn you. I am a sleigh (wagon) driver from the village of Lilikova. You and your family must escape tonight. They will be rounding up all the Polish citizens from this area and deporting them to Siberia. I am to be one of the drivers of those sleighs that will be taking you from here to the train station."

Helena hurried home. Wladyslaw Brodacki didn't believe her.

"Why would they be throwing us off our land? This land is deeded to me. I have papers! Besides, where are we supposed to go?"

Unfortunately, Tadeusz felt that because he wasn't an influential person of any great stature, nor was he a landowner, that there wasn't any need to be concerned. Kloczkowicz had warned him that it was no longer safe for any of the Polish people in the village and had been feeding Tadeusz secret information in addition to verifying all those "rumors" Tadeusz had been hearing. Despite all of this, Tadeusz felt that there was no safe place for them in all of Poland. If they had no place to run to, then why should they bother? Besides, where could they go with a four-week old infant who needed to be kept warm? This was winter. He figured it was better to brave the future, and whatever it might bring, than to brave the elements.

He should have heeded Kloczkowicz's warning, but for these reasons, he didn't. At 2:00 a.m. on February 10, 1940, there was a pounding on the door. The Russian Security Police had arrived.

"Open up, we're here to interrogate you! Get up against the wall! We will be relocating you to another region."

The soldier had a complete list of names, property, and the vital statistics on all of them.

"You must leave everything. This land no longer belongs to you. All the kulaks (independent farmers) must leave everything behind. A Russian family will take over your home and all of your property. We will allow you to take some clothing, only."

They quickly packed a bag with clothes and diapers for the baby. There was no time to pack everything they would need, even had the soldiers allowed it. They did not own a trunk like the one the Brodackis owned. The uncle and aunt quickly packed theirs with food, clothing, and valuables. In the rush, Helena left her wristwatch, which was the only good piece of jewelry she owned, but she did pack a few mementos, photos, money, and their passports and documents. She dressed in the best clothes she owned, and then packed a few cloth diapers and blankets.

She begged the soldier to allow her to make some tea for her four-week old baby. The abscess had affected her breast milk, and she was worried that it would harm her child. Geniusz was crying for nourishment but the NKVD would not allow it. Within 40 minutes, everyone in the village (anyone who wasn't Russian) was outside being ushered into the sleighs. All their friends and neighbors were there with them. The police had also rounded up lumberjacks and other people employed in forestry services (regardless of their nationality). They were needed for slave labor in the forests of the Siberian gulags where timber was cut for railroad ties. The nurse from the

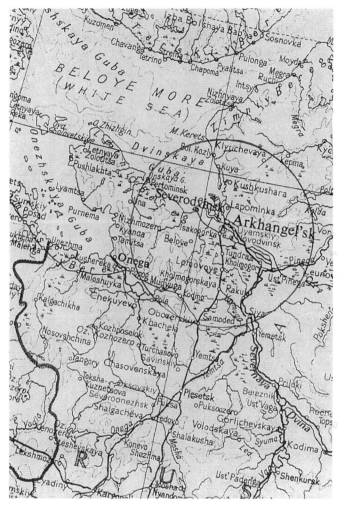

Map of Russia and Arkhangelsk Camp

hospital, Dumanski, was among the detained citizens. She didn't even have a single bag with her. They took from her house with just the clothes she had on her back. Others were treated even worse. Several people had cuts and bruises to show for their slowness or resistance.

It was nearly dawn when Helena asked if she could be allowed to see the doctor for the injection she required. She would need to do something quickly because of the pain she was experiencing. The guards told her that they wouldn't allow her to go to the clinic unless she left her baby behind (to insure her return). An armed guard then accompanied her to the clinic and the sight of the two of them frightened the staff. However, for some reason, the doctor said he couldn't give her an injection because there was an inflammation in her breast. Helena believed he meant that the injection might cause the infection to spread. She was too frightened to really concentrate on what the doctor was saying. The doctor, true to his profession, was angry at the inhumanity of the soldiers.

"You can't deport a sick woman. This is cruel and inhuman. You are injuring a child in the process."

The guard lied.

"Don't worry; we're only transporting the undesirables (Polish landowners) to Kobrin. She can get looked after there—in their new residence."

The transport would lead them further away from their home than Kobrin. The Szelazeks were on the first sleigh in the long procession from Dywin. They were headed for a train that would take them to Siberia.

Kloczkowicz was standing in the center of town, scanning the sleighs as they passed by. He spotted Tadeusz and his family in the first sleigh. Visibly distraught, he shouted as they drove by.

"I warned you! Why did you stay?"

Tadeusz waved to him and shouted back.

"Don't be upset, Kloczkowicz. Do you think there's no God in Siberia? We'll survive! We'll be all right!"

☞ 14 ☜

Travelling to Siberia

You will leave the country of your birth—Poland.

The night was cold. Helena wrapped Geniusz more closely in the heavy blanket, trying to give him a feeling of security. She felt nothing. Fear was numbing her senses more than the cold. The long line of sleighs moved briskly along the hard-packed snow as they made their way toward the train station. Kobrin looked like a ghost town. People were hiding indoors; hoping the sleighs would pass their homes without stopping.

As their sleigh rounded a sharp curve in the road, it lost its balance and tipped over, tumbling everyone into the snow. Geniusz was flung into a snowdrift but fortunately was not injured. His thick, heavy blanket had cushioned the fall. Everyone was wet and cold as they picked up themselves and their belongings out of the road. Helena begged the driver to let them stop at the nearest house. She needed to change and feed her baby who was crying loudly. The crying must have touched something in the driver because he walked up to the house and pounded on the door. The frightened inhabitants cracked open the door and he ordered them to let the mother and baby into their home. Helena quickly changed and nursed the infant. Minutes later, they were back on the road and the nightmare continued.

In town, the train was waiting for the prisoners and more armed Russian soldiers appeared. They controlled the crowds, sorting and shoving people into the wooden cattle cars of the train. Each was packed with up to 80 individuals; then the doors were locked shut. The boxcars were so crowded that the deportees had to stand up for most of the time, taking turns lying down and sleeping. It took the soldiers all day to fill up the trains. All day they spent without food, water, or bathroom facilities. The fear, exhaustion, hunger, and the stench were torture. However, it could be argued that at least these people were lucky. They were not meant to be exterminated like those prisoners, both Polish and Jewish, who were held by the Germans. These people were political prisoners, undesirables, but they were also a valuable resource for Communist Russia.

The deportees were military or police personnel, politicians, people associated with foreign correspondence, and so on. They could be people who either traveled frequently or who had direct correspondence with foreign state representatives. (Something as simple as a relative in America could get a person deported.) Other deportees were individuals who followed occult studies, Red Cross workers, refugees, smugglers, ex-members of the Communist Party, priests, active church members, the nobility, landowners, wealthy merchants, bankers, industrialists, even hotel and restaurant owners. All these people were to be used as slave laborers to construct a stronger Russian empire. An entire system of "corrective" labor camps covered most of Russia. According to statistics published by Zbigniew S. Siemaszko, the night the Szelazeks were pulled out of their home was the start of the February 1940 deportation of 220,000 Polish citizens. It was the first of four major deportation waves that forced 1,492,000 people into slavery.[3]

Tadeusz and Helena were among those who were headed to the Northern Special Purpose Camps in the White Sea and near Arkhangelsk on the mainland of Siberian Russia. Among the prisoners in their group was a rich Byelorussian woman named Tamara. She was on a list of arrested individuals who were scheduled to be deported along with the Poles. Apparently, she had been inconvenient to some local official. (It was rumored that she had been his mistress and was now out of favor with him.) She kept insisting to any Russian guard who would listen to her that there was some mistake. She hated the Poles just like they (the Russians) did. The Poles were bad people and she never had anything to do with them. Surely they couldn't possibly be sending her into exile. There had to be some great mistake. Unfortunately for her, there was no mistake and her remarks managed to alienate her from the other deportees. She learned about intolerance and injustice first from her own people, then from her fellow travelers.

Another Byelorussian fellow, named Dekiesz, was actually boasting to the Russian guards that he had killed more Poles than they had. He felt that they should release him since he had done such great deeds for his country. One guard finally said to him, "Well, it's good to know we're deporting some deserving criminals along with these innocent Polish people."

---

3 Sword, K. (*Deportation and Exile: Poles in the Soviet Union, 1939–48*, London 1994, p26). Quoting statistics from Siemaszko, Z. S. (*W somwieckim osaczeniu*, London 1991, p.54).

Dekiesz's fate was a little different from that of the rest of the travelers. The Russians took him to a Soviet labor camp (for Russian citizens) where they worked him to the point of collapse. When they finally released him a year later (an acquaintance later related), he took off with his family to parts unknown. He feared reprisals by any of the Polish residents in their town for his admitted criminal acts.

Despite the cruelty of that night's deportation, at least the Poles, Jews, and other minorities who left that night were given an opportunity to live. If they could survive the harsh environmental conditions and hard labor, they could live and maintain some kind of family unity. The unfortunate people of Finland, however, suffered much more greatly at the hands of the Russians than the Poles did. They were often dragged naked or poorly clothed from their homes and were allowed to freeze to death. The Russians, for the most part, viewed the Poles as free labor or, at worst, as farm animals. However, they at least fed, clothed, and gave medical aid to the Polish laborer. They gave them as much consideration as they did their work animals, which were necessary.

The trains arrived at the Stolpce station where the prisoners were off-loaded and transferred to a Russian train. Tadeusz was allowed to buy some milk and water for the family. (He was given such freedom because, officially, he was not classified as an exile. He was not on the list of deportees but had chosen to accompany his wife However, by the time he made the purchase, the train was leaving without him. In a panic, he ran to the stationmaster and asked him if there was any express train that could catch up with the prison train.

"Are you crazy man? Shouldn't you be running in the opposite direction? That train means your death!"

"My family is on that train. My wife and child are my life. I am not a dog, and even a good dog remains faithful to his family."

So he purchased a ticket for an express train that, eventually, caught up with the deportees in the next major town in Russia. Tadeusz actually got there before the slower moving prison train. He was waiting for his family with a few of the much-needed supplies when it finally arrived.

Meanwhile, back on the prison train, the guards began questioning Helena as to the whereabouts of her husband. If she had knowingly aided in his escape, she could be treated badly. Her husband had been allowed to accompany her to Siberia. He was not, however, allowed to leave whenever he wished. He had to ask permission.

Her aunt, Bronislawa Brodacki, was yelling loudly in the background so that the guards would hear her.

"He escaped! He ran away! He left his wife and child and ran away! The coward, to leave us all behind like that! He could have taken us with him!"

The nurse, Domanska, was also in the same cattle car with Helena. She spoke several languages and said in her perfect Russian dialect, "He loves her. He would never leave them. It's obviously an accidental separation."

Helena was thankful for Domanska's presence. It helped her remain calm; and it was reassuring to hear someone else say that Tadeusz would never leave her. Her faith in her husband was strengthened when she saw him standing on the platform at the station. The officials checked his name on his papers and compared him to the names on the manifest, then locked him into the cattle car with the rest of his family.

The trip to the north took several weeks. Russia is a huge country with so much land that a person could travel for days and see only one building. This fact didn't give much hope to the prisoners as they looked out of the cracks in the planking. Even if a person could escape, where would they escape to? Most of the people were in no shape to escape in the first place. They were cold, starved, sick, frightened, and, worst of all, many had already died along the way. The very old, very young, and the infirm couldn't stand the harsh conditions and were the first to die. However, others just gave up and willed themselves to die.

The train would stop every two days, or so, whenever the transport came to some small town. The exiles would get some hot water and a little broth made of fish, or rice, or scraps. They would each get 200 grams of bread. If you had money, and someone at the station was willing to sell it to you, you could buy real food. Some people tried to hold on to their money at any cost, some to their own demise. However, starvation wasn't the real threat that frightened everyone. It was the cold. The temperatures would drop so low at night that a person's hair would freeze to the floor and plank walls when they fell asleep.

The train's destination was the settlement camps near Arkhangelsk on the White Sea. The trains passed Minsk, Smolensk, Moscow, then up to Vologda and the outskirts of Arkhangelsk. The trip took much longer (longer than it ordinarily should have) because every few days the train would stop in the middle of nowhere and wait. Sometimes they would wait for a whole day. Helena passed the agonizingly long periods of inactivity by studying the Russian Cyrillic alphabet with Domanska. This activity proved to be of great help to her, on more than one occasion. The ability to read and write, in more than one language, was crucial for the survival of displaced people. It meant the difference between life and death. You wouldn't live, if you couldn't communicate the need for basics—like bread.

Tadeusz, on the other hand, always managed to find something to do. However, not always was this an intentional pursuit on his part. Again, he narrowly missed the train and was nearly left behind. Seeing the train pulling away from the platform, he ran till he was able to jump onto the back rail. There he spent most of the day, standing on the coupling, waiting for the train to make a stop. Although this was a cold and frightening experience, he had an opportunity to observe how trains were connected and how they could be climbed while in transit, which became invaluable knowledge in the future.

During this transit, Helena realized she was seriously ill from the infected abscess. It was oozing pus and if it wasn't before, it was now affecting the breast milk. This in turn caused constipation in her baby, as there was no other nourishment other than the infected breast milk. Geniusz cried continuously from the pain in his stomach. Although doctors were allowed to walk among the prisoners and examine them, they did not treat anyone very extensively. They were not carrying any medicines with which to treat patients. Naturally, they didn't have anything they could give Helena for her discomfort.

The doctors were basically there to identify, and separate, the dying from the living. Dead bodies were left behind in stacks alongside the tracks. Those who lived shared the belongings of those who died. Food, however, was still scarce. The Brodackis refused to share any of their food with the Szelazeks. Apparently family ties did not extend to their niece, her husband, or their grand-nephew, which was awful because the large chest the Bro-dackis had packed carried enough food to feed them all.

A Russian soldier was listening in on a conversation between Helena and her aunt during one of the stops. Helena asked for a little food. All she needed was enough to keep up her strength, at least for Geniusz's sake, even if the aunt could not see it in her heart to keep Helena alive.

"Hey old woman, can't you see she's sick and can use some food?"

"I'm sick; I need it more than she does!"

The Russian guard had a little raw meat that he had just bought for himself and so he offered it to Helena. She thanked him and took it, even though she knew that eating the meat raw would be almost impossible for her to do. The meat did freeze rather nicely in the unheated car so they were able to eventually trade it for some bread. The guard's humanity and generosity was greater than that of Helena's own relative.

Caring for the baby was a nightmare. Whenever they were allowed to get off the trains and use water, she would hurriedly rinse some of the three or four diapers she was carrying. Then she would quickly wipe off the baby, and put on a dry diaper. The reason the diapers were dry was because she would press all the newly washed cloths against the warmth of her skin. She would use her body heat to dry them. She prayed that God would protect her from pneu-monia as she shivered from the cold, wet material against her body. Helena kept her baby as clean and dry as pos-sible, but it was more of a miracle than anything else that the child was surviving the ordeal as well as he was.

The temperatures in the Arkhangelsk region of Sibe-ria can reach -30 degrees Fahrenheit. The climate is inhospitable to man, yet there was a reason why the Russians built settlements there. They needed access to a seaport for trade and shipping routes. Ivan the Terrible had established the seaport of Arkhangelsk (the first Russian seaport) on the White Sea. Apart from its importance as a seaport, the region was especially famous for its forests. It had the largest wood processing plants in all of Russia, and it was here that the prisoners were assigned to work. A lot of wood was needed to keep the war effort going and, therefore, large numbers of laborers were needed. The scenery was pretty enough, with its untamed forest wilderness and miles of rivers; but the beauty was marred by danger. Wild animals and treacherous tundra terrain kept the prisoners from venturing too far from the train tracks while they surveyed the Russian landscape. The Northern Dvina River flowed past Arkhangelsk emptying into the White Sea. Many other small rivers flowed into the Northern Dvina, one of which was the Kinga. This river, and Kinga Lake (Kinga Ozoro) in Archangelsk's tundra region, would be the destination of the Szelazeks.

The deportees eventually arrived at the train station in Kholmogory. From there, groups were divided and carted off to different areas. Some of the deportees were sent on further east, into the depths of Siberia. Two of the wagons were to go to a settlement only 14 km away. It was called Vodopad (Waterfall) in the district of Pleshetsk. Among the group going to Vodopad were the Szelazeks and Miss Lotka Domanski, the nurse. Also Miss Danka Jaworska was in their group. She had been joined by her fiancé, Wolski, who also willingly left Poland just to be with her. (They were married in Siberia.) The guards purposely disconnected the two wagons, in which this small group was, so that they would be diverted to the Kinga River settlement.

The Russian guards had become almost solicitous toward this small select group of exiles. They had even formed friendships with the younger deportees of those two wagons. After their rounds, they would often stop by to spend the evening joking and laughing with the group. The guards were just as cold, cramped, and miserable as their charges. They needed some amusement to break up the monotony. Leaving these two wagons off the train was their way of giving the deportees a little advantage. The settlement camp in this area was known to be a little more humane than those in other places in Siberia.

While officials were processing the paperwork on the new arrivals, the guards took Helena and her baby to a clinic in Arkhangelsk. Another woman, who was also in need of medical attention, accompanied them. Helena had no money, so she wasn't sure how she could purchase medical supplies if she needed any. She quickly realized that the trip would produce no positive results. All the nurses at the clinic in Arkhangelsk seemed more interested in her clothes than her complaint.

"You look so warm in that nice Polish coat. It must be very cold were you come from. None of our Russian women wear coats like that."

This was very true. The poverty was so severe in Russia that people wore thin overcoats on top of layers of ragged clothes. They couldn't afford, or find, coats like the one she owned. To the Russians, the Poles were wealthy.

Just as Helena feared, the trip to the clinic was definitely nonproductive. They told her that they needed to cut open her breast to drain the abscess but all their surgeons were gone. There were no more antibiotics, gauze, or bandages available anyway. Helena realized that they had no qualified doctors or specialists to perform simple operations. At the moment, all the doctors were elsewhere busy caring for the injured Russian soldiers coming in from the front lines of Finland. There were no forms, or paper for that matter, on which to write down a request for a specialist. Basically, there was nothing they could do for her.

The baby was still in distress, but they could do nothing more for him than to give him some warm tea. Geniusz hadn't had a proper bath in weeks so at least Helena was finally able to wash him. They also allowed her to sleep in the corridor since they couldn't admit her. But basically the entire trip and separation from Tadeusz was a both a hardship and a waste of time.

The next morning Helena, the baby, and the other woman were told to go back to the train station from where they had come. Of course, now there was no transportation that would take them to the Kholmogory train station. And, since they also had no money to pay for a carriage, they had no choice but to walk across the frozen river. On the way, they met a Russian man who offered to pull them on his dog sled, if they had a kopeck or two. When he found out they were Polish, broke, and on the way to the settlement camps, he told them to run away.

"You'll die there. 10,000 have died there already. There were 300 priests in the first camp. They're all dead now."

He pulled them to the nearest village for free. The two women asked the people at the village if anyone could give them money for a ticket. No one would even consider giving them a loan. Helena began to despair at the situation she found herself in.

"Everything that belonged to my family has been taken away by Russia and still it's not enough. No one here will even extend me a seven ruble credit to take me to prison!"

The local population was not allowed to give directions to any deportees. Giving directions to a prisoner might assist them in an escape. And, if there were an escape (and a local civilian was involved in any way), they would be shot along with the escapee. So, it was up to the two women to find their way to the prison camp where their families were taken. Helena was thankful that she had started studying the Cyrillic alphabet with Domanska. She painstakingly read the signs until she located the name of the camp on a signpost.

They were ready to begin walking in the direction of the camp, when a Russian soldier gave them a suggestion that could help them. He told them to find a certain house in which some foreigners lived (he didn't specify their nationality). Apparently they had helped people who had found themselves in financial difficulties. He said the Red Cross maintained the house. (Many Red Cross workers were deported to Siberia along with other altruistic groups. And, even there, they manage to extend aid to others.) If the two women wanted to get in touch with them, they'd have to cross the river again. By this time, Helena was totally exhausted and feeling sick. She could no longer carry the baby. So, the other woman volunteered to go across by herself and try to get aid for all of them. Helena thankfully remained behind and, as she lay down on a bench to rest, she prayed that things would work out. Perhaps the people no longer lived there, or perhaps they couldn't give them any money. All she wanted was to see her husband again.

The soldier, who gave them the information, sat down near her and started talking.

"I was in that part of the country you're from. The Byelorussian girls looked beautiful with all the ribbons they wear, like your Polish Krakowianki. Everyone was rich in Poland. All the boys had bikes. Such wealth! But I found out that those Byelorussians are not like us real Russians. I even liked the Polish people better than those Byelorussians. On the way through your part of Poland, the Byelorussians greeted us with flowers. They said we were saving them from Polish domination. Then, when the Germans attacked us, they turned their backs on us and joined the Germans. They no longer greeted us with flowers, they greeted us with pitchforks! They thought the Germans would be their allies, give them independence and their own country. Turncoats, all of them! Now I feel that, maybe, the Polish people aren't as bad as we were told."

He gave Helena a roll and some sugar. Then he showed her where she could buy some food if those foreigners across the river gave them any money.

"I'm being sent out to the front to fight. They'll give me some food but I'll be more cold than hungry."

"I'll give you my warm coat for seven rubles. No one here has one as warm as this."

"No, you'll need your coat. I'd gladly take your coat, but you'll die faster from the cold than from hunger."

As it turned out, there was no need for her to sell her coat. The woman came back with 18 rubles that the Red Cross people had given her. They could use 12 rubles for transportation and 6 for food.

Dawn arrived and the train station began to show some signs of life. Helena and the woman found the stationmaster and asked where the group of exiles, which had arrived two days ago, had been sent. He consulted his lists.

"Some were dropped off at Kholmogory and some were sent to Chomogorki. Which one are you interested in going to?"

"Kholmogory."

"Are you sure it isn't Chomogorki? If it's Kholmogory, then the group was sent to a camp 14 km away. If it's Chomogorki, then that's a settlement 310 km away."

At this point Helena burst into tears. Both places sounded the same to her and she was no longer sure to which one Tadeusz was sent. She had enough money to get to the camp that was 14 km away but what if it was the one that was 310 km away? She was separated from her husband, and she was alone with her baby in a strange country where she couldn't even communicate properly.

"What are you crying about? We have plenty of husbands here, lots of work to do, but no women, so you're in luck. You are good looking and you'll find a man in no time," the stationmaster said.

His words, so easily spoken, brought home the chilling reality of what was happening all around her. Once separated, many wives never saw their husbands and families again. Fortunately for Helena, the closest station was exactly the location she was looking for and it was only a short ride to the settlement. The other woman was not so lucky. The official told her that her husband and children went on further east. Helena never did find out what happened to her. Perhaps she never did find her way back to her family. Helena prayed that this didn't happen to the woman who had been such a great help to her and Geniusz.

The next morning she arrived at the settlement camp, Vodopad. Tadeusz had already been assigned to a single men's barracks because he had refused to stay with the Brodackis a minute longer. His hatred for the Brodackis was more intense than ever. They were more his enemy than any foreign invader could ever be. The young couple had received more kindness from people who were supposed to be their enemies than from their own relatives.

The chief of security at the camp (an interrogation officer for the NKVD) was named Stefan Palkin. It was his duty to interrogate Helena upon her arrival, to review her papers, and to assign her to her barracks. Palkin assigned her to a "family" house where Tadeusz would be able to join them later. She was told that the commandant's name was Loginov. This settlement was a government run camp filled with a mixed assortment of deportees. Originally, groups of exiles would be dropped off in the middle of a forest, handed an axe and told to start building their shelters from the cold. If they didn't build something quickly enough, they'd freeze to death. Another nearby settlement was a *kolhoz* or cooperative of regular civilians. They had to live off of whatever they grew, or raised, and they didn't get any government subsidy. (They were actually envious of the prisoners and their "supported" status.) Making a living off the land was particularly difficult since the Siberian terrain is basically tundra. The growing season below the Arctic Circle is short and the land is swampy when the spring does arrive. Only the Eskimos, whose paths would often cross those of the settlers, didn't seem to be affected by their bleak surroundings. They'd come into the settlements on their reindeer-driven sleighs to trade for food or goods.

A few weeks after arriving, Helena had an opportunity to watch a group of Eskimos as they followed a huge herd of reindeer. One of the Eskimo women needed to go into their store for supplies. She carefully dug a hole in the snow near the sleigh, put her baby wrapped in fur and sealskin into the hole, and then covered it with snow. She then went into the heated building. At first Helena was shocked, but then she realized that the snow was acting as insulation against the cold, and that the baby was as warm as if his mother was holding him. The Eskimo's reluctance to bring the child in could have been an effort to protect him from diseases brought on by the overheated dwellings of the foreigners. Because of these diseases, Eskimos always kept their contact with outsiders to a minimum. Helena watched as another Eskimo searched through the trash looking for any useful objects. It amazed her how they had adapted to their cold, bleak surroundings. They didn't seem to need a house for protection in the same manner that the deportees did.

The house to which the Szelazeks were assigned was a barracks-type dwelling that was divided by corridors into four sections. Each section was further divided into four areas. A total of sixteen families lived in each barracks. The Szelazeks shared one of the areas with an old Ukrainian woman named Lavrynjuk.

During the interrogation and processing, Stefan Palkin asked Helena why she and her husband were there. The name Szelazek was not on the official list of deportees, only Brodacki was. She explained that Mrs. Brodacki was her aunt and that she was serving as a farm hand.

"So, your aunt and uncle have officially adopted you?"

"No. But, it was understood that I would inherit the land someday."

"That still doesn't make any sense. There was no reason for you to have accompanied them here to Siberia. Your names aren't on the list and your aunt must have known this. Had they insisted that you were only working on their land, you would have been left behind. You would have gone home to your parents, particularly since you were married and no longer dependant on your aunt. The Russian government had no intention of exiling the Polish working masses, only those rich individuals who exploited the poor. In this case, it's the Polish landlords on Russian territory who were the exploiters."

His statement was a shocker. Still, Helena did not believe that there was anything she could have done differently. Certainly this whole deportation experience couldn't have been avoided. Could her aunt have saved her, but chosen not to?

The Szelazeks set up their cots and meager belongings in the building to which they were assigned. Among the few objects that Helena had brought with them was a rolled up picture of the risen Christ with the dedication of their family's life to the Sacred Heart of Jesus. They hung this picture up on the wall over their bunks, unaware of the regulations barring the display of holy pictures, crucifixes, or other religious objects. Nothing of this sort was to be hung on the walls of Russian settlement camps. There was no room for God in the Communist Party, and no form of religious expression was allowed. However, after having just lost everything that belonged to them, including their homeland, the only thing Helena and Tadeusz had left was their religious expression. So, in this new home of theirs, surrounded by other prisoners, they hung up the relic.

During the first inspection of the barracks, the security chief, Stefan, noticed the picture on the wall.

"Who put that picture on the wall?"

The old Ukrainian woman, Lavrynjuk, promptly spoke up.

"It's theirs; they're responsible for putting it up there."

Stefan turned to Helena and spoke with her.

The Relic

"Does He help you?"

"Yes, Sir . . . . Does He bother you?"

"No."

The chief turned and spoke to the old woman who was listening intently to the conversation.

"Why do you think that man was crucified?"

"Because he was a criminal and an enemy of the state!"

The chief burst out laughing at her.

"Durak (You fool)! Don't you know anything? He was a leader of an oppressed people. He despised capitalism and the corrupt monarchies that owned a man's body, and mind. His aim was to gain equality for everyone. He was the *first communist!* We are the second communists! Now get out of here, you stupid old woman, while I interrogate these comrades."

When the old woman left, Stefan turned to the stunned couple who had been prepared for the worst. They had expected a brutal punishment of some sort. Instead, the security chief put his finger to his lips and then pulled out a small gold medal with the image of the Virgin Mary on it. This was a symbol of his belief in the Russian Orthodox Christian religion. He wore it under his uniform, away from the prying eyes of others.

"This was given to me by my precious mother whose memory I will always cherish. She taught me her religion and I will never forget her, or give up my faith. You can teach your little one, as my mother taught me. Just don't be obvious about it. Take down your picture and remember this is not the place to practice your religion. Keep our conversation secret. You will die if you betray me. I work at this job to feed my family, but I won't jeopardize their welfare for you. I respect people who stand up for their faith . . . for what they believe in. But be wise, discreet, and you'll all manage to live through this exile."

When he left, the two looked at each other in disbelief. Here, in exile, they found that God and religion did exist. Just like Tadeusz had shouted to Kloczkowicz—"Do you think there's no God in Siberia?"

One of the first things Helena did, when they were finally settled in, was to look for medical attention. A woman named Baszow applied a heated flax seed oil preparation on the abscess. (This flowering plant was grown in the camps and used for a variety of purposes, primarily to relieve ulcers and constipation in farm animals.) The homeopathic remedy worked. It drew out the pus and destroyed the infection. This experience led Helena to study as many folk remedies as possible; this knowledge, in turn, helped everyone around her over the years. Throughout most of her life, conventional medicines were not always available, affordable, or convenient during emergencies. Homeopathy always gave her an alternative to helplessness.

It was customary, in settlement camps, for babies and small children to be left in the care of a camp-run nursery while the mothers went to work in the forests with the men. The prisoners were assigned to a variety of jobs: some were assigned to lumber cutting details, groups were told to remove brush from the land, to build roads and dwellings, and to provide materials for the war effort. After working in the forests during the day, the deportees were encouraged to create homes for themselves. They were expected to plow fields, grow vegetable gardens, set up group kitchens, and buy farm animals. The Russian officials hoped that once the people settled down (with a piece of land of their own to farm and raise animals on), they'd want to stay in Siberia of their own free will.

Since baby Geniusz was not even four months old, Helena had the option of caring for him personally until he was at least six months old. Then she would be required to leave him in the nursery. During the assignment of duties, Stefan asked her if she were aware of the recent conversation he had had with her aunt.

"Your aunt says she's too ill to work, although she doesn't appear to be ill. She says she can take care of your child and that you can go to work in her place."

That was the last straw. There was nothing wrong with her aunt. Once again she was trying to use Helena as a workhorse, even in this Siberian prison.

"The child is *mine!* I am breastfeeding my son and, according to your rules, I have the rights of a new mother to be with my child."

Stefan Palkin smiled.

"Now I understand the relationship you have with your aunt. This shows to what ends your aunt would use you. It explains why you're here and not back in Poland. So, when you're ready to take up your assigned duties, just let me know."

Working in the Siberian forests as a lumberjack is a dangerous, difficult profession. Nearly every day there was an accident or death among the workers. The majority of prisoners had never cut down a tree before they arrived in Arkhangelsk, and the inexperience was killing them. Most of the heavy labor was being done 7 km away, in a wooded area called Volosne. There, the prisoners were cutting down the forests, building barracks, and setting up a new settlement. In order to get to Volosne, the workers had to walk down a footpath along the Kinga River and then cross over the frozen river. Heavier objects were transported by boat or, if the river was frozen, by sleds. It was a lot of backbreaking work. Eventually the workers made a crude bridge across the Kinga to lessen the dangers of crossing the fast-moving river or falling through the ice. Many Polish prisoners lost their lives to nature and the wilderness.

⇌ 15 ⇋

Life in the Camp

"Your enemies will be plentiful throughout your life, as mushrooms after the rain. But like mushrooms, you can step on them and crush them into insignificance.

Life fell into a routine. Tadeusz was assigned the duty of clearing out brush and branches in the forest. This was considered "light duty" since cutting down trees with primitive hand tools and removing the stumps was much harder. This light duty was assigned to him because of a recent accident at the camp. A horse had kicked him in the stomach and had caused a hernia; so he was grateful for the lighter duty. It was some time before Tadeusz could carry anything heavy; and often Helena would help him whenever it became necessary. She would carry the larger limbs or purposely take the heaviest weight of the tree upon herself. She did whatever she could do to help him meet his (quota) obligations. However, his good fortune to have this unexpected assistance, gave rise to envy among some of the other prisoners. They feared that he would be given preferential treatment since everyone seemed to like him. He was treated with respect and consideration even by the guards.

There were two fellow inmates who were determined to eliminate Tadeusz. They were Dempczuk and Prus, whose duties were food delivery to the officers and the camp kitchens. This was also considered light duty in the camps. Therefore, they feared the rise of any competitors who could possibly take away their cushy jobs. To them, this Szelazek character looked like a threat that needed to be eliminated.

One day, they filed a false reported that Tadeusz was inciting the workers to mutiny because he decided to walk off his job, without permission, and was even now sleeping in his barracks. The chief of security, Stefan, called Tadeusz into his office. It was his duty to investigate all the formal complaints and to deal harshly with prisoner rebellion. So, he needed to get to the bottom of this report.

"Did you walk off the job today? Did you know that you can be executed for inciting disobedience in our workers through your dereliction of duty?"

"I was ill with a fever and couldn't continue working. So, I told the guard that I was going to the barracks. I was in bed when you summoned me."

"You are required to report your illness to the camp doctor and then get permission to leave. Now I have to make you spend the night in the holding pen. I have no choice in doing this. It is the designated punishment for the crime. Not knowing what the regulations are is not an excuse in this camp. It will be cold and cramped in the box, but you should be able to survive. Prisoners are usually thrown in without blankets or protection from the weather; but I won't put you through that. I'll provide you with some blankets. You must learn from this experience and follow regulations to the letter. Be careful of other prisoners. The fact that you've been exiled together doesn't make you comrades."

Somehow Tadeusz survived the freezing cold of the night, despite his fever and illness. This incident served as a good warning to Tadeusz. He was learning the ropes, and the rules, of the games being played at this camp. There were enemies here who he had to be wary of— enemies who could cost him his life. As Stefan said, just because a group of people find themselves in a prison and guarded by a common enemy, doesn't make them friends. He now knew they needed to be cautious in all aspects of their present lives. You didn't have to "do" anything to make an enemy in a prison camp. Sometimes you just had to exist.

At one point, the work camp of Lesopunt in Korbaty (30 km from Kinga Ozioro) needed workers to produce their quota of wood for the war effort. The commandant of that camp, Ogarkov, requested workers from Vodopad and Tadeusz was among those who were lent out. He was there for nearly three months and the working conditions at the camp were dreadful. He knew that if he didn't get back to Vodopad, he would be finished off here and would die separated from his family. The lack of food and the abuse the workers received were intolerable. When the designated time was up, Tadeusz thought he and the other loaned prisoners would be returned to their camp. However, Commandant Ogarkov had changed his mind. He decided the workers were still needed at his camp, so he held on to them hoping the loan would be forgotten. Tadeusz was assigned to forest detail when he brought up the subject of their release from duty. The overseer to whom he spoke told him that the only place he was going to be released to was to his grave. Apparently, the commandant of this camp would routinely work his prisoners into an early grave. Tadeusz would not let that be his fate. He flew into a blind rage and beat the overseer senseless; then took off through the ancient woods in the direction of Vodopad.

The forest was a dangerous place. He wasn't especially concerned about the bears, Siberian tigers, wolves, and other ferocious animals, however. Humans were far more deadly. The terrain also posed a problem during his escape. The forest floor was covered by tons of debris and fallen trees. The rotted vegetation was so deep in some spots, that falling into pockets of this matter was like falling into quicksand. To make matters worse, there were bogs with actual quicksand throughout the tundra. Entire lakes could have a mat of grass and weeds, thicker than a carpet, covering the surface. A person could push a six-foot long stick down through the mat and never reach the bottom. It was small comfort to Tadeusz that, if some vicious creature was following him through the forest, it also risked falling into a pit from which it could never get out.

While he was travelling, Tadeusz kept thinking of the story he had heard circulating in the camp. A woman told him about her sister who had lost her voice, and some of her mind, after being stalked by a bear. The woman had been picking berries in the forest, not far from the settlement camp, when she encountered a large brown bear (perhaps a grizzly). By the time she saw the bear, it was too late. It grabbed her by the arm and she passed out from fear and pain. When she came to, she realized that she wasn't even seriously injured, but that the bear had dragged her to a nearby cave. Then when she tried to leave, the bear would come to the mouth of the cave and chase her back in. It never wandered too far from its lair and whenever the woman tried to leave the bear would be back in an instant. The cave became both a prison and a refuge for her. The psychological strain however, was too much. She lost her voice and couldn't even scream for help even though a well-used path was near enough to run to. She would walk slowly outside, pick a few berries with the ever vigilant bear eyeing her suspiciously; then, if she tried to walk too far from the den, he'd bound toward her forcing her back inside. After several days, the woman heard a small vehicle on the nearby path. She knew they would be looking for her so she decided to make a run for it. The driver was shocked to see a disheveled woman running out of the trees followed by a bear. The situation was extremely serious because the driver had no weapons, only a wagonload of straw. So, he lit clumps of straw with a match and kept throwing the clumps at the bear, which eventually gave up his pursuit of the woman.

Now Tadeusz was alone in the woods, off the beaten path. Yet this was safer than being discovered by the guards who would soon be looking for him. Whenever possible, Tadeusz would stay on the road, leaving it whenever he heard the search party coming after him. In this manner, he was finally able to get himself back to Camp Vodopad. He immediately reported to the commandant and told him about the appalling work conditions in the camp, and the fate of the other prisoners loaned out. This abuse of the exiles (and more importantly, his workmen) angered Commandant Loginov who sent a formal demand to Ogarkov. He requested the immediate return of all of his men without any excuses.

Loginov was a decent man and a noble enemy. This seems a strange thing to say about someone who should have been despised by his prisoners. However, everyone can appreciate a man of integrity. The commandant cared for the welfare of his prisoners. There was food, medical attention, and fair treatment for the Polish exiles in his camp. He was an officer, doing the job he was assigned to, and doing it as impartially as possible. However, when a Pole got involved in some trouble, or made a grievous error, the punishment was less severe than that inflicted upon a Russian. This was because, according to the commandant, Poles were ignorant of the customs and laws of Russia. However, should the Pole make the same transgression a second time, he would be shown no mercy.

Unlike some of the Siberian prison camps established exclusively for criminals, it was possible to earn money in the settlement camps despite the fact that money was in short supply. A person could do odd jobs, make crafts, and sell things to the nearby residents of the kolhoz. The Szelazeks took every opportunity that presented itself to better their conditions. Through hard work and frugality, they were finally able to purchase their first real acquisition. They bought a goat to provide milk for Geniusz. This was a necessity because the price of milk was extremely high and the owners of dairy animals were not always honest. Helena had been cheated in milk purchases on a number of occasions. She had traded her only good, expensive quilt for a daily supply of milk from a neighbor's goat. The woman gave her milk twice; then she refused to give Helena any more. The agreement had been verbal so there was nothing Helena could do about it. So, Tadeusz sold his fine wool suit (which he had just acquired as payment for cleaning outhouses) to purchase a goat. And now that they had a goat, they also needed to construct a proper pen to house it.

Tadeusz received permission, from the officer in charge, to go into the nearby village to get shingles for the little roof he was putting on the goat pen. He hadn't been gone for more than an hour when one of the prisoners by the name of Yamarkier went to Stefan's office. He reported that Szelazek wasn't working and should be punished. (This deportee was actually a neighbor of Tadeusz's from his hometown). Stefan went to the commandant and told him how this man, Yamarkier, wanted to get Tadeusz into trouble. Stefan had already questioned the officer in charge, so he knew Tadeusz had received permission to leave the camp. The commandant allowed Stefan to arrange a confrontation between Yamarkier and Helena. Stefan summoned Yamarkier to his office and then left him alone with Helena. She asked the man why he was so interested in Tadeusz's whereabouts. Why was it any of his concern whether Tadeusz worked or not? Weren't they all prisoners here in the same camp? What was the purpose of reporting Tadeusz's absence to the authorities? Then she informed him that Tadeusz had received permission from the officer in charge to leave the camp. Therefore, if he felt he was being cheated somehow (by not seeing her husband punished or injured), he could tell her exactly what it was that he needed from them. Perhaps she could oblige him. In the future, she informed Yamarkier, she would keep a very close eye on his whereabouts. He never troubled them again.

Life continued on in the same stressful manner; however, an incident eventually occurred that changed

Tadeusz's job assignment. There was a Ukrainian man by the name of Szefczuk who was running the camp commissary. One day, Tadeusz noticed that the man seemed upset. Szefczuk knew that Tadeusz had owned his own store before his deportation, so he confided in him. He was worried about the inventory. Apparently, the inventory didn't match the supply records and other purchase forms. To make things worse, there was to be a review by some officials and he was worried that they would accuse him of incompetence, or perhaps even theft. Although ration cards were used to purchase most goods, some purchases were made with money. He could be accused of embezzlement. That could mean imprisonment or, if the commandant wished it, an execution.

As a former storeowner, Tadeusz gave him some advice and encouragement. Szefczuk was a good man but not especially good at managing a store or at bookkeeping.

"Don't worry. Conduct an inventory of all your supplies before the officials get here. You may find that there are fewer discrepancies than you suspect. Then, go back to your records and make adjustments in the supplies records. Wherever possible make the new records and receipts look authentic."

Tadeusz gave him a run down of some accounting procedures that would make the corrections and adjustments legal; and simultaneously, save his neck. Szefczuk was grateful. The officials arrived shortly thereafter, and to Szefczuk's relief, the review went over without a hitch. Eventually, Tadeusz was asked to work in the Volosne store as a bookkeeper. Such a job was ordinarily assigned only to trusted personnel of Russian origin, or to specially privileged civilians. It was upon Szefczuk's recommendation that Tadeusz received his new position.

There was another incident that involved a Russian man, named Igorov, who lived in a nearby kolhoz. He often spoke with Tadeusz and looked forward to exchanging jokes with him. During the late spring, he was rowing a boat over the Kinga River. The ice had melted but the water temperature was still freezing. Igorov spotted Tadeusz working along the shoreline and he began waving. The greeting was a little too vigorous, and somehow he lost his balance and tipped over the boat. Igorov wasn't much of a swimmer and the heavy clothing dragged him down to the bottom. Tadeusz threw off his jacket and shoes, and jumped into the river. He pulled Igorov to shore and then proceeded to save some of the supplies that had fallen out of his boat into the water. They built a fire as quickly as possible and dried off as best as they could. Exposure to cold water could be fatal in Siberia, even in the spring. They had to get back to camp quickly before their body temperatures dropped from the dunking experience. Tadeusz had risked his own life to save Igorov's life and his property. Naturally, the heroics did not go unnoticed with the camp officials.

Tadeusz made many friends among people who should have been his enemies. He did so by treating them as he wished to be treated. The Russians called him a variety of names. Often it would be Zielezniak or Sielazak or Slezak since the pronunciation of Szelazek seemed difficult for them. However, most people simply knew him as "the actor."

The commandant's wife found Tadeusz, and his antics, especially entertaining and charming. She called Tadeusz "the artist." Sometimes he would walk down the road toward his job in the forest (infested with ravenous mosquitoes), wearing a hat of his own construction. It had a veil around the brim like a beekeeper's hat. As he passed the commandant's house, he would often greet Mrs. Loginov by picking up his hat and twirling it in a kind of comic salute. The veil would splay out as it twirled making her laugh at his appearance. She looked for occasions to talk to him (the boredom of living in a settlement was as bad as a prison sentence for many people). Then, during one conversation, she found out that he had done some acting on stage. From that time on, Tadeusz was asked to use his acting talents to entertain high ranking guests and officials at the commandant's quarters. His excellent memory, flair for the arts, and courtly manners had finally paid off. He was often excused from work at the store to spend time entertaining the commandant's guests. An added bonus was that they allowed him to eat some of their "gourmet" food. (Whatever they ate was always better than what was being served in camp.) Sometimes they would even let him take a little of the leftovers home to Helena and Geniusz.

Tadeusz recited the prose and poetry of famous Polish writers to the guests. He performed soliloquies and one-man plays, as well as impromptu satirical poetry about prominent political figures. The guests' favorite satires were usually those about Stalin. They would roar with laughter as Tadeusz irreverently turned Stalin into a paranoid, bumbling idiot. No one at the camp could have guessed what was going on at those parties, let alone how the average Russian official felt about Stalin. Tadeusz was as discreet as usual and kept their private conversations to himself.

It was interesting to see that even though there was supposedly no class distinction in Russia, in reality, there was still an inherent class structure. The commandant once joked about it.

"Although we are all equal here, we still have three classes of people in Russia: Good, Better, and Best. Our leaders, on the other hand, try to maintain our equality by strict economic measures. Perhaps you heard their old saying, 'What's yours is mine and what's mine, don't touch!'"

Commandant Loginov proved to be an intelligent, sophisticated man who appreciated talent and education. The fact that he was an excellent officer was unusual. It was hard to find good officers in Russia because of previous Communist purges in the ranks of the army. They had slaughtered most of the educated people, especially the Russian nobility, many of whom had been officers in the army. As a result of the purges, the Russians had problems finding good leaders who could get them through a war without destroying the country and the people.

Mud and water were everyone's enemies at the camp. Keeping one's feet dry was a constant battle. There was a chronic shortage of rubber boots and waterproof foot gear. This fact especially endeared Tadeusz to Loginov's wife when he managed to fix her white rubber boots. She had mentioned how badly they leaked and how difficult it was to get new footwear. So, Tadeusz soaked pigskin in gasoline till it became a gelatinous sticky substance. Then he cut pieces of rubber from old tubes, adhered the pieces to the boots with the rubbery, waterproof mass he had created. Then, as the gasoline evaporated, the pieces stuck firmly together. The boot repair was a success; thus his reputation as a Jack-of-all-trades began. It seemed that there was nothing he couldn't do.

There was a Russian officer in the camp who was in charge of stacking cut timber that was used for stoking the furnaces, boilers, and other machinery. Some of the lumber was also sent out to be used for railroad ties, buildings, and materials at the front lines. Every lumber camp had a quota to fill for the war effort. This officer had the men stack the cut wood in an area that was easily accessible. The wood had been arranged in two huge stacks that were the size of small airplane hangars. When the spring thaw came, the frozen ground began to melt and the wood settled deeply into the mud. The officer had not realized the area he had chosen was such a swampy mess because he had been new to the camp. Activity in the area churned up the ground, until the workers could no longer get at the wood. The area had turned into a sea of mud. Wagons were mired hub deep in a muddy swamp and work slowed down to a crawl.

Tadeusz was coming back from an errand in Premylov (35 km away) when he saw the officer pacing back and forth. He was holding his head and moaning.

"I'm a dead man. I'm a dead man. Szelazek, I can't supply the wood fast enough from these cursed piles. I hadn't thought that the ground surface would swamp up so badly when I laid out the piles of lumber. If we don't meet our quota of wood this week, I'm a dead man. If I can't supply the quota, they can ship me out to the front lines, or shoot me for being such an idiot. Our commandant will be punished as well, if we fail."

"Don't be upset, I can help you. I'll move all this wood for you in two days. Just supply me with the manpower I need."

"I'll give you whatever you need. Anything, just name it."

Tadeusz procured many wide planks of lumber, which he fastened to large squared blocks of wood, thereby constructing a floating, wooden sidewalk across the mud. The sidewalk acted like a bridge connecting the mud-mired wood piles. He instructed two strong men to load up wheelbarrows and wagons with lumber, while two other men took turns pushing and pulling the wagons across the wooden sidewalk. Another team of men stacked the contents of the wagons onto solid ground. Then another set of men brought back the wheelbarrows and wagons to be reloaded. Following this procedure, and working around the clock with a constant fresh supply of workers, all the lumber was moved within two days. The quota would be met and disaster was avoided.

A few days later, Helena happened to be picking up some supplies from the commissary when Stefan Palkin came in. He greeted her enthusiastically.

"Good morning to you, Mrs. Szelazek. I just heard of the "rescue" mission. That Szelazek is a character! When he doesn't want to work it's like getting milk from a male goat. But, when he wants to, he can produce 200 percent over the quota."

He looked over at the store manager.

"Hey there, Comrade Szefczuk, give Mrs. Szelazek ten meters of satin material and ten meters of linen."

Then he loaded Helena down with the unexpected treasures.

"These are just a token of everyone's appreciation."

Along with their regular (non-paying) assignments, Tadeusz and Helena took on any jobs that could earn them some money. They cleaned the outhouses, removed the excrement, and used it for fertilizer. This particular job paid 60 rubles, which was a week's pay. Unlike some of the other "nobility" who said they'd rather die than be so degraded, they did whatever they could to exist. And while some of the other prisoners waited for English and American soldiers to save them, the Szelazeks worked on saving themselves. Several hundred deportees died in the camps during the first year. Some gave up hope, some starved, some froze, and others got sick and died. Some prisoners refused to work at any cost. They didn't plant their own private gardens with vegetables or prepare for the coming winter. They freely, and with full knowledge of the consequences, chose starvation over life.

The Szelazeks, however, prepared a small garden that they fertilized and tended in their spare time. They were lent a horse and wagon on which they loaded manure that they used for the fertilizer. They worked this fertilizer into the soil of the garden and planted potatoes. It produced a remarkably large number of potatoes for the size of the garden. However, their gardens produced problems along with the bountiful crops. Other inmates of the settlement were constantly raiding it. Unfortunately, the thieves did not dig up the potatoes; rather, they would yank them up by the stalk, destroying the plant in the process. Even more potatoes could have been produced if the thieves had had a little consideration.

Tadeusz decided to make an announcement to everyone in the camp. He told them that, although the garden was his, he understood their need for food. However, he would prefer that whoever was stealing his potatoes would at least dig them up. Upon hearing of the thefts, many of the other prisoners and farmers denounced the thieves and said that whoever it was should be killed. However, this wasn't Tadeusz's intent.

"You can replace a potato with money, but you can't replace a human being."

Shortly thereafter, a guard caught a woman stealing from the garden. Rather than having her punished, Tadeusz told the authorities to release her. Stefan, as chief of security, warned the woman to leave the garden alone. He told her that she was setting a bad example for the rest of the inhabitants of the camp. He was disgusted with her lack of ethics and her laziness. This woman was capable of working and could plant her own garden if she chose. She had no children to care for, unlike Helena, who worked and had an infant. But the woman refused to listen to the chief's warnings.

"They have more food than they need, and I will continue to walk into their garden and take what I want."

Unfortunately for the woman, within a few months, she would not be able to walk at all. She was boarding a moving train, which was packed with newly released prisoners, taking them out of the camps to freedom. She did not want to wait for the next transport, so she tried to jump onto the moving train. She slipped and fell under the wheels losing both her legs in this tragic accident. When the other prisoners heard of the amputations, they all reminded Tadeusz of her arrogant words. Now she wouldn't be walking anywhere, let alone into Szelazek's garden. She would remain in Camp Vodopad, forever at the mercy of others. Tadeusz never wished any harm to befall her, or anyone else, over something insignificant like potatoes. God, however, exacted a harsher punishment than anything Tadeusz could have expected.

❧ 16 ❧

Geniusz

Despite the horrors, harsh climate, and the ugliness of
war, not everything was unpleasant in this land of
exile. The Szelazeks were blessed with a wonderful son.
Their little Geniusz was growing into a beautiful, intelligent child. He was extremely gregarious and everyone
loved him. He was able to bewitch everyone he came
in contact with. The old Ukrainian woman Labrynjuk
used to play with him and call herself his grandmother.
Even the commandant would take walks with him, holding the little boy in his arms. He was passed around the
camp, from person to person, like a mascot. Geniusz was
a big, strong boy for his age. He was extremely agile and
learned to speak early. What was most unusual about
him was that he was extremely perceptive, seeming to
know things that he was never taught. By the age of nine
months, he was not only able to walk but also to dance.
By the time he was a year old, he began reading.

Tadeusz suggested to Commandant Loginov that he
institute Sunday as a day for family socials. He suggested
that by creating this atmosphere of fun, shared interests,
and concerns, a bond could be created between prisoners
and guards alike. Loginov agreed to the plan. He allowed

people to put on plays and have dances. These activities immediately brightened up the dismal atmosphere of the camp. Whenever the music played, little Geniusz would dance his little heart out. He'd make everyone smile with his enthusiasm.

One beautiful spring morning, he was walking with his mother when he saw a rainbow. He stopped in his tracks, put his hands up to the sky, and with a deeply emotional voice he said a prayer.

"Bozia, Bozia (God), please bless Mamma and Tata and give them happiness and health."

Helena was startled and a chill seemed to settle within her. She had never taught him to say such a prayer. She felt the hair on her neck rise.

"Why don't you ask God to bless you, and give you good health too?"

"Oh, well, if I have to. God give good health to Geniusz too."

His reaction was very unsettling and it stayed in Helena's mind.

Time passed and he continued to amaze everyone. They called him a genius and everyone told the proud parents that they were truly blessed to have a son like him. There were so many examples that demonstrated his growing awareness and intelligence. A man named Alinski lived next door to the Szelazeks. He usually left his key in the door but, one day, he noticed that it was missing. So, he stopped by to ask whether Geniusz had perhaps taken it to play with. The little boy said he did and said to follow him. He took them far down the road through the camp and there he stopped, looked at a spot in the dirt, dug down, and picked up the key. He knew exactly where he had left it.

He loved little toys (of which there were very few since people didn't have time to make them). His favorite was a little tiny hinged box in which Helena kept her rosary beads. Geniusz called it his "puki." One day, some older children took his little box and substituted a wooden hammer for it. They told the little one-year-old that that was how you traded for things. But he didn't want their hammer. He ran home and told his mother that they stole his puki and left a "kuj, kuj" (he didn't know what to call the hammer). Geniusz showed Helena where the big boys lived and she talked with their mother who returned the box. It was a remarkable feat of intelligence and strength, that a small child could manage to stand up to children who were years older than he was.

It was a gypsy woman (one of many who had been deported as an undesirable) who told Helena not to be too happy with her son's progress.

"Your son is not growing and maturing like a normal child. He is growing by the day, the way other children are growing by the year. He will not live long."

Helena was shocked. How could the woman say such things?

"So, what you are saying is that only stupid children should be allowed to live and mine should die because he's smart?"

"It is not because he is smart that he will die. He was not meant to live long and he knows it. He is fitting in as much life as he can into the time he was given. Do not be overcome with grief when he dies. "

Helena felt a chill deep down inside her soul. Intuitively, she knew that the gypsy was right. She burst into tears but decided it was best not to tell Tadeusz what the woman had said. She had no idea that Tadeusz had heard the same prediction, five years earlier, from someone else.

Food and goods were plentiful until Germany attacked Russia on June 22, 1941. After that, it was difficult dealing with shortages; however, availability of food was not always the answer to staying alive. The camps were always plagued with a variety of illnesses. It was a primitive, dirty place, and the food preparation area was never hygienic. The building where the people purchased their food was never as clean as it should have been. People frequently became ill from diseases like dysentery and other intestinal ailments because of eating there.

Helena became ill with some sort of intestinal ailment. She couldn't keep down any food and it appeared as if no food was passing through her intestines. She was taken to the hospital in Premylov where she was kept for a week. Tadeusz was working on the day that they took her, so he was not made aware of the situation. Geniusz was supposed to be looked after by the neighbors until Tadeusz's return that evening. However, no one was looking out after the child. They had left him entirely alone for eight hours. So, 15-month-old Geniusz decided to search for his mother. He started walking down the camp road until he spotted a woman. She looked like his mother from the back. So, he followed her. He kept calling her, "Mama . . . Mama!" The woman finally looked around and recognized him. He was so disappointed that it wasn't his mother that he started crying and headed out down the road again. The woman stopped him and took him back to his barracks; only to find that the room was empty. When Tadeusz returned that evening, the woman told him all about the little boy's efforts to find his missing mother. As for Helena, the doctors found the source of her illness, which was a blockage in her intestine. It eventually passed, and she was able to return home a week later.

Then, not long after that incident, another crisis entered the Szelazeks' lives. There was a serious outbreak of dysentery in the camp. Geniusz contracted the disease, which immediately resulted in constant diarrhea. Helena had no idea how to help him or what to feed him to help get rid of it. Whatever they tried didn't seem to work. The camp doctor had no medicine to give him. All the clinics in the area were depleted of medicines because of the number of people who were ill. Then the deaths began.

Helena was distraught. Geniusz had been sick for one week already and he wouldn't be able to withstand much more suffering. His little throat was collapsing like a person getting ready to die. Tadeusz also got ill, and now Helena was caring for the both of them. She was worn out and terrified. As she sat exhausted and crying on the edge of Geniusz's bed, he woke up and spoke to her.

"Please mama, don't cry. Go to sleep. Nothing, but nothing, hurts me anymore. Just give me the picture of Bozia (God)."

She handed him the picture they had hung on the wall near his bed, and he fell back to sleep. Toward morning his breathing stopped. Helena started screaming in anguish and somehow Geniusz roused himself again. He opened his eyes, smiled at her, and died.

The camp doctor was upset that he did not have anything with which he could treat Geniusz. He did not want to be there when the baby died, so he had left camp two days earlier. He had to get away from the sight of the little boy, whom everyone had loved, and whom no one could save. The little genius's life was over at the age of 16 months.

Helena was devastated. She wanted to die or go into mourning forever, but even that option was taken away from her. She had to deal with the reality of life around her; after all, Tadeusz was still sick with dysentery. Then she had to deal with the man who was supposed to be tending her goats. He had taken the money but was neglecting the animals. She also had to talk to the coffin-maker about building a coffin for Geniusz. Even though the chief coffin maker for the camp was paid a salary for his duties, he was always demanding extra bribes from the families of the deceased. He requested 30 extra rubles from Helena. Naturally, she didn't have that kind of money, but she asked if she could pay it later. He refused.

"If I don't get my money, I'll make a coffin for him like a box for a dog."

This was too much for Helena. She flung herself on him like a deranged animal. She scratched at his eyes, she bit, kicked, punched, and released all her anger and despair on the beast. Her baby had died needlessly and this monster wanted to discard his little dead body like that of an animal. She went straight to Commandant Loginov, crying her eyes out. He fired the man from his job; then he ordered the coffin maker's replacement to create the finest coffin possible. Geniusz was buried on a hill with a little wooden cross marking his grave. Helena buried him with his beloved puki toy.

Geniusz died on August 15, 1941. It was three days later that the prisoners were informed of an amnesty decree that had been issued on August 17th. The term amnesty was insulting to all the innocent Poles who were ripped from their homes and turned into slaves. The term seemed to label them guilty of some crime for which they were being pardoned. Nevertheless, this decree meant freedom for them. The Poles were free on August 18, but little Geniusz had died a prisoner. Perhaps, if the amnesty had been declared just a few weeks earlier, Geniusz could have been saved. Had circumstances been different, they might have been able to take him to Arkhangelsk, or some other regional hospital, where they had medicine. But, fate had not decreed it to be so. He died and was buried in the only place he had ever known as home.

Helena became ill from crying for hours in the cold rain at the cemetery. She had a bad cold, but still she kept kneeling, praying, and grieving over her son's grave. She did not want to leave the body of her son behind. She wanted to bury him back in Poland with all the rest of her ancestors in their family plot. Stefan asked her what she would do with the body as they traveled, how would she carry it with her? She eventually saw the futility of her desire. She had to accept his burial in Siberia, knowing that she would never see him or visit his grave again (in fact, it was possible that no one would ever be able to find his grave, even if someone was able to return there).

An acquaintance of theirs, who left the camp at a later date, reported that Stefan Palkin was often seen stopping by the little gravesite on his rounds. She felt at peace knowing that, at least for the time being, someone was looking after her son's grave in her absence.

∽ 17 ∽

An Offer Declined

You can be wealthy if you so desire, however, you may choose not to be.

As mentioned, the Sikorski-Maisky Pact freeing the Poles was signed on August 17, 1941. Sikorski, the Polish Prime Minister, had opened negotiations with the Soviet ambassador to London, Ivan Maisky, to re-establish diplomatic relations between Poland and the Soviet Union. Joseph Stalin agreed to the pact and released tens of thousands of Polish prisoners-of-war held in the Soviet camps. The Soviets granted amnesty to many Polish citizens, from whom a 75,000-strong army (the Polish II Corps) was formed under General Wladyslaw Anders.

This new amnesty created all kinds of problems for the Russian settlement camps. The Russians could no longer legally hold onto their workforce, so many NKVD personnel never released information about the amnesty. As a result, some Poles finally heard the news months after others had been released. This was because the camp leaders feared a mass exit. After all, many of these camps consisted mainly of Poles and prison guards. If the Poles left, all the NKVD guards would be reassigned—possibly to the front. These guards wanted to avoid this at all costs. So, it was in Russia's best interest to convince (or prohibit) the Poles from leaving.

Word came down to all of the Polish deportees in the settlements that they could leave Russia, but only if they joined the army to fight off the invading Germans. All those who wished to leave would be transported to Uzbek S.S.R. (Uzbekistan) where an army of two infantry divisions was being mobilized. The immediate families of the soldiers were allowed to accompany them to the mobilization site. The prisoners of the Vodopad Settlement jumped at the opportunity to leave Siberia, despite Commandant Loginov's disappointment. He had thought that all the deported Polish people were settling in nicely, starting a new life in Russia for themselves. And now, everyone was petitioning to leave . . . including the Szelazeks.

Commandant Loginov was going to miss Tadeusz and his wife's company, and he told them as much. He had come to depend on Tadeusz's insights and quick wit; now that they were leaving his settlement, he was saddened.

One evening, he visited the couple and made them a proposition he hoped they would not turn down.

"You will be presented with an opportunity to return to Poland, after the war, and to take over a prominent political position. I have already talked to a friend of mine and told him of your abilities and your value to our government. The new Polish government, which we are setting up, will need 'our people' in all the key positions. I have also informed a number of officials that I recommend you to help with the transitional government in Poland. My country has no intention of allowing Poland to be totally independent. Russia does not intend to release anything it owned prior to the conflict with Germany. Regretfully, there is nothing anyone of us, including myself can do about that. Anyway, there's no sense in worrying about that right now."

"How can you be so sure that Russia will win this war or that you'll be allowed to set up your own government in Poland?"

"Russia is not giving up, Stalin is not giving up, and soon they'll have the support of the Allies, so it's inevitable."

"So you're proposing that I go into politics. But I have no training in politics."

"We will train you and when we're done, you can have any position you want. You'll have enough money to clothe your wife in furs and jewels. You can have your weight in gold. What we need is a man who can talk to his fellow Polish countrymen . . . a man who can lead them. We need to convince them that only through cooperation can we begin to rebuild. Our two countries will be stronger, and better, now that we can unify our governments. Stalin's vision is to build a strong nation that can resist, and crush, our mutual enemies. But, we will need true leaders, men with vision, men with the ability to move people with their speeches. I've seen how the other prisoners look up to you, listen to you, and trust in your integrity."

Then he turned to Helena, trying to get her to convince her husband.

"You'll be the wife of an important dignitary. Life will be easy for you, no more starving or rags to wear. You can have a family and educate your children at the finest schools. This is something to consider, no?"

"It's my husband's decision. I will stand by what he decides."

Tadeusz was silent for a long while, his forehead resting on the palm of his hand, deep in thought. Finally, he answered Loginov.

"I know you have made this offer to me with the best of intentions, since you are an honorable man. Russia is your homeland and you are dedicated to its survival. But, I am Polish and I will never make a life for myself built upon the backs of my brothers. Poland is my homeland and even though Stalin has plans for absorbing our country to make a stronger Russia, I cannot be a part of that. You say that the change is inevitable, that the Poles have rarely been masters of their own land, but you forget that the Poles are never subjugated for long. Even if you forbid them to speak their language, change their names, take away their homes, they will always be Poles! Even if I take this opportunity and use it to do some good for my countrymen, which I know is your intention although you have not said so, my people will see my actions as a betrayal. It is because I have integrity that others can trust me. I prefer self-imposed poverty if it means I keep my honor intact. I have given this enough thought and I graciously decline your offer."

⁓ 18 ⁓

Waiting for Deployment in Uzbekistan

Your sons will all die…

In September 1941, the freed Polish prisoners who wished to join the army to repel the German forces were allowed to leave Russia and were transported across thousands of miles to Kubyshev in the Novosibirsk District, and then on to Guzar in Uzbek S.S.R. (Uzbekistan). According to estimates, less than 10 percent of the Polish people who were originally deported ever made it out of Russia. This means that either several hundred thousand deportees remained there, or they were no longer alive.[4]

It was already November when the Szelazeks left Vodopad. Unimaginably, the train ride out of Siberia was worse than the trip bringing people into exile in 1940. On the way in, at least initially, there had been food, of sorts, given to the prisoners, and some people had had money with which to purchase it. Now that the Russian government felt no responsibility to supply the freed prisoners with provisions, there was no food and no money. Only train passage was provided. The newly freed status of the Poles did nothing to endear them to the starving Russian

---

4 Sword, K. (1994, p. vii).

populace who had to remain behind. Many Russians felt that it was Poland's responsibility to feed her own citizens, so they would not aid the Poles in their journey to freedom. Bands of Soviet criminals often preyed upon the weak refugees, sometimes murdering them for a handful of coins.

The same cattle trains that had brought them into the wilderness were now taking them out. The crowding was not as great, but then there weren't as many of them now. These recruits for the Polish Army, and their families, arrived in Kubyshev in a state of complete exhaustion. They were sick, starved, louse-covered, and looked more like animals than human beings. They had traveled 2,500 miles with an anticipated journey of another 2,500 miles to reach Uzbekistan. To Tadeusz, starvation seemed their most likely fate. He had seen the bodies of diseased, starved exiles littering the railroad stations. He knew he had to do something before they died of starvation too, and the situation became even more intense when Helena realized she was pregnant again.

Tadeusz used his cunning and agility to form a workable plan. First, he removed a board in the floor of the train. Then he crawled out of the hole while the train was still moving. After pulling himself up and along the outside (or across the roofs) of the train, he got to the supply wagon. He undid the latch, slid open the door a crack, and got inside. Once inside, he took small amounts of flour and supplies from the bags, and then stitched them back up again. He got back to his own wagon in the same fashion had gotten to the supply car. Tadeusz accomplished this tricky feat on several occasions. Each time he would share the small amounts of supplies he had retrieved with the other deportees.

The guards finally sealed the wagon door, thinking that would prevent someone from removing the supplies while they were stopped at the stations. The seal didn't stop Tadeusz for an instant. He was able to open the seal, and after he picked up more supplies, replace it while in transit. However, he realized that he would soon have to stop the foraging missions as it was becoming more dangerous with the heightened security. He once again shared the food, gave away the flour, and kept a white flour bag for himself (as a substitute for a much-needed suitcase). This arrangement didn't seem to suit a man named Mankowski who wanted to fight Tadeusz for the flour bag. Just before any blows were thrown, a man named Kwiatkowski quickly jumped between them, pushing Mankowski away with a curse.

"He gives you food, which he risked his life to get, and you begrudge him the bag it came in? While he saves your life, you abuse him and his generosity!"

Mankowski was not to be deterred. He felt he could do as well as Tadeusz, so he made his way through the hole and over to the supply wagon. There, he broke the seal on the door and stole a noticeably large amount of supplies. Of course, Mankowski couldn't fix the seal on the door, so he left it in an obviously damaged state. Naturally, the theft was discovered and after that, an armed guard was stationed inside the wagon at all times. Everyone lost out because of one man's stupidity and greed.

The exiles arrived in the Uzbek and were dumped unceremoniously in the middle of nowhere. They had to make their way to the nearest recruiting station by foot. The camps were scattered over vast distances (some as far away as 900 km). The Szelazeks' destination was a station close to Guzar district, Bukhara. They walked toward a nearby town and were able to spend the night in a local *czahajna* (tavern). They slept with all their clothes on and with their heads on top of their suitcases to prevent the locals from stealing everything. They were awakened, in the middle of the night, by the screams of a man whose shoes were being ripped off his feet by a thief. The climate of southern Uzbek was subject to extremes in temperature, and choking sandstorms were also frequent. The country, and its scenery, was odd looking compared to what everyone was used to. In some areas, there were large, ugly salt fields that had been strip-mined. Other areas had fields with strange-looking cows of a breed the Poles did not recognize. The horses were beautiful, while the sheep had huge, fat tails the size of plates. The language that the inhabitants spoke was odd and did not resemble Russian at all. All the old insecurities returned when communication became impossible.

Helena was finally able to find a room to rent in the village nearest the recruiting station while Tadeusz went with the rest of the men to the encampment. On this day, May 15, 1942, Tadeusz formally joined the Polish Land Forces. Polish enlistees were now arriving by the hundreds. They all looked forward to being trained and shipped out of the Uzbek, and out of the Russian's clutches.

Ironically, although there was danger all around them, it was a tiny, little insect that posed the worst danger. Lice overran the country and its people. Helena had never seen such huge, hybrid, nasty looking things. She and Tadeusz would pick diligently through their clothing, trying to keep their things as free of them as possible, but all their efforts were to no avail. It was sometime during the days following their arrival that Tadeusz was bitten by a diseased louse and contracted typhus, which was becoming epidemic at the time. The fever came upon him quickly, and he was sent to the nearby hospital. The building was already filled with people suffering from malaria, typhus, and dysentery.

When Tadeusz was admitted to the hospital, he was wearing his best clothing: a new jacket and new shoes. The state of his dress was apparently important to the staff of the hospitals because they seemed to have segregated the patients into two groups. The well-dressed patients were admitted into rooms within the hospital. The impoverished, ragged patients were lying on the ground outside the building. Desperate, dying people were begging for water there. They were covered with filth, and most had dysentery as well as typhus. When Helena came to find Tadeusz at the hospital, the sight of the sick overwhelmed her. It was not in her to pass by another human being in agony. So, as she searched for Tadeusz in the hospital, she carried water in the palms of her hands to help the parched victims lying on the ground. At this point, Helena was already seven months pregnant, and she knew was running the risk of getting infected. But, it was impossible for her to walk away from these dying people without trying to help them. The Guzar region was becoming one mass grave, and the living were turning their backs on the dying to save themselves. But Helena knew that sometimes even little acts of mercy could keep the human spirit strong and the will to live alive. She did what she could for both those who were struggling to live and those who were very obviously dying.

Despite all her efforts, her search for Tadeusz was fruitless. Finally, a couple of days later, she was informed that Tadeusz was no longer at the hospital. They had

From Exile to Eden

moved him to Kitabo with the rest of the seriously ill soldiers. Kitabo was located 4 km away. She ran the whole way and found him, still alive, but in critical condition.

Tadeusz had been hospitalized for almost four weeks when Helena's landlady decided to throw her out of the rented room, because she was afraid she would be exposed to typhus. It was a natural reaction, but one Helena could not sympathize with, especially in her advanced state of pregnancy. A second Uzbekian woman took her in, but this new landlady proved to be a thief. She stole a number of things before Helena moved her meager belongings. She continued to sleep at the thief's house, but she kept her luggage at the house of the first landlady. Eventually, she found a Ukrainian woman who owned a house in the village. This woman agreed to rent her a room for 100 rubles a month. That was an exorbitant fee considering the size of the accommodations. Nevertheless, it gave her a permanent address. Without a permanent address she would not be able to keep in contact with the army and the army hospital. However, more importantly, without a permanent address, she ran the risk of being shipped out and deposited in some other part of Russia. As a vagrant, she could be put back into a settlement camp to earn a living. This happened to some women who lost husbands or fathers and therefore had no money or further connection to the mobilizing army.

A sergeant in the Polish Army advised her to raise some much needed rent money by selling Tadeusz's overcoat. It was in excellent condition and would bring a good price. He even offered to sell it for her. Although she didn't know him, her need for money outweighed caution. The sergeant did sell it; however, he pocketed most of the money for himself. Helena felt betrayed by her countryman, but the small amount of money that she did receive helped her in numerous ways.

Helena waited for an update on Tadeusz's condition. She was terrified for herself and her unborn child. It was possible that she could be left alone to deal with this nightmare if he should die. Days passed and still, no word. He was not listed among the dead, but he was not returning home among the living either. To make matters worse, it was forbidden for civilians to travel between towns without a pass; the authorities were trying to curb the spread of disease by limiting travel. This meant Helena was unable to look for him.

The Ukrainian landlady saw how much Helena was despairing over the situation, so she advised her to go to the policeman who stood guard on the road outside of town. She told her to put money into his pocket first and then beg him for a pass to Kitabo. He would have a harder time denying a request if the money was already in his pocket without asking for it. A bribe in the right pocket never hurt in Uzbekistan.

Helena walked up close to him, and in a flirtatious manner, slowly slipped the money into his pocket. As she did so, she quietly whispered, "Please, can you possibly give me a pass to Kitabo? My husband has been gone for four weeks and I have to know if he's still alive."

"Okay, I'll write you a pass, but you'll have to go to the steam baths to get disinfected. Everyone is supposed to hand them their clothes but, if you do, they'll ruin them for you. They usually burn all the clothes instead of disinfecting them and then they hand you some rags. You'll have to slip the woman in charge five rubles and she'll slide your clothes through. You'll have to give them money on the way back, too."

The guard had shown no surprise at her request, so this type of bribery was obviously commonplace. Her only concern was that there would not be enough money (from the sale of the coat) to pay everyone off. After putting aside money for the bribes, Helena used the rest for some wine, raisins, and eggs to feed Tadeusz at the hospital. She got through the checkpoint with no problem and walked to Kitabo. Unfortunately, when she arrived there, they told her that he was no longer in that facility. She should check at the next hospital. So, she checked at the next hospital, but he wasn't there either. This was too much for Helena. She began to cry, as overwhelming fear encompassed her. Now she was terrified and all she could do was continue walking and searching for her husband.

Fortunately for Helena, she could speak Russian fairly well and was already picking up the Uzbekian language. After hours of searching, Helena finally found Tadeusz in a tent among a group of bedraggled people. The people turned out to be soldiers who were recuperating from typhus. They were about to be shipped out to another camp where they would recuperate further.

Tadeusz was weak, thin, and worn out, but alive. The nurses told her how very sick he had been and how they had spoon-fed him. They admired her clothes; and she understood why they were so attentive to her clothing when she finally saw Tadeusz. Helena almost didn't recognize him. Various staff members in the hospitals had taken all his good clothing away from him. She gave him the food and stayed to chat with one of the doctors. He told her to come back the next day so that she could travel with Tadeusz to his new location.

The distance was too great to return home for the night, and she didn't have enough money to go through the chain of bribery the next day. Helena spotted a tavern nearby, and decided to spend the night there. However, it was filled with convicts who were newly released from Russian prison camps. It was more than likely that among these patrons were thieves, murderers, and rapists. They were certainly a grubby, lice-covered crowd, so she thought it would be safer for her outside. She gave the innkeeper five rubles for a chair that she propped up against a wall outside of the building. She sat there talking, purposely keeping herself awake all night long. The innkeeper kept her company for part of the night, so she felt a little safer.

Finally the night was over and she arrived at the hospital. There stood Tadeusz looking worse than a beggar. Thin rubber boots were tied on to his feet with some rope. Instead of a shirt, he wore a hospital gown. Ripped pants were also tied on with a rope, and a blanket served as a jacket. She had never seen him so miserably dressed before. But, he was alive and the reunion was sheer happiness.

The train took them both to a recuperation unit in the army camp. Helena saw him get settled in and then started her long trip back. The military camp had no provision for visitors or family members, and because a chair propped up against a wall for five rubles was no longer in her budget, Helena had decided to return to her rented room. It was that night that she began to feel sick and feverish; she had a slight cough and was extremely exhausted. When she finally got back to her room, she felt like she had the worst cold of her life. The next day the landlady helped her get to the hospital where they started to treat her for a cold. That was when they found the red spots on her body, which meant typhus. She had been bitten during her search for Tadeusz, and now she was sick, eight months pregnant, and alone in the hospital. There was no way to get word to Tadeusz.

The fever made her delirious—at one point, she was sure her mother was there, visiting her. She remembered her mother bringing some apples from their orchards. However, all the nurses said they never saw her mother, but the conversations she experienced were so real, she was sure they were mistaken. Those were the good moments. The rest of her illness was nearly unbearable—it was filled with pain, heat, nausea, and diarrhea. She was sure she would die and never see her husband again. She became despondent. What was this life all about, anyway? She had so few moments of happiness. Her life had been one constant test of her strength and religious beliefs. Everything and everyone she loved was gone or missing. And then the hallucinations started again.

The devil was picking up the edge of her bed and shaking it furiously.

"Get off this bed! Get off now or I'll smash you and this bed against the wall!"

"Where am I to go?"

"Get off this bed or I'll smash your head against the wall! Now!"

So she got out of bed and sat down on the one across the room. She sat there until a nurse asked her why she wasn't in her own bed. Helena refused to go back until the nurse put a light on in her corner of the room. The devil seemed to stay away when the light was on.

It was a long time before she realized that she was no longer pregnant because she kept going in and out of consciousness. Eventually, the nurses told her that a baby boy had been born; he had lived for a short while, and then he had died. They had disposed of the child's body in a mass grave, somewhere in the vicinity. She had no choice but to accept the hospital staff's word for it. Helena had wanted to christen her child, and it hurt her deeply that this had not been done before the body was disposed of. She had planned on naming him Marian. She and Tadeusz had wanted another son, and now, this one was dead as well. She would never have an opportunity to see him, to see his eyes, or to remember his face, and thus she had no closure. She kept wondering if he was truly dead. Perhaps her son still lived and someone stole him to sell him in the slave markets that still existed in these countries. Maybe he'd grow up and never know he had a mother and father who loved him. These thoughts tormented her even after the fever disappeared.

~

The Polish army was being mobilized to ship out to Iran (which was still called Persia at that time). One group of soldiers had already shipped out in March and April, and Tadeusz was to be transferred out with the next group that was leaving in August 1942.

Tadeusz had located Helena at the hospital, but the last he had heard was that she was not going to make it. He knew he couldn't leave without knowing for sure, however. If she remained behind, he knew it was unlikely he would ever see her again. Tadeusz had already lost two sons and he couldn't bear the thought of losing his wife as well.

One day, the soldiers were standing in formation, being instructed in final preparations for boarding the transport, when Tadeusz stepped forward. He disregarded protocol and addressed Colonel Rezinski directly.

"I have a request to make of the Colonel. May I be granted permission to speak?"

"What is it soldier?"

"I do not want to leave my wife behind. She is lying unconscious in the hospital, on the verge of death, and I have to be sure of her safety. I can't leave here without knowing if she will follow me in the next transport."

"So, you need to drag your woman around with you instead of fulfilling your duty?"

"What did you say? My wife is no vagabond slut that I just happen to be dragging around. She is my sacramental partner in life. I demand an apology for your insult to my wife! I am ready to do whatever I have to do to have my wife with me."

Colonel Rezinski was astounded at the exchange. No soldier ever defied him so vehemently before. This soldier could be facing a court-martial, but he was not backing down.

"What exactly are you ready to do?"

"I'm ready to rip off these rags (he pointed to his uniform and the stripes)!"

The insult to the uniform was not lost on the colonel, but he let Tadeusz continue.

"Okay, soldier, calm down. Were you ever in the army before this enlistment?"

"No sir."

"Step back into formation, soldier."

Then he signaled to a lieutenant.

"Lieutenant, let me see you in my tent for a moment. Have these soldiers wait."

Everyone was shocked. Surely Tadeusz would get court-martialed for his outburst. He had just insulted the uniform, insignias, and (indirectly) the country that the uniform represented. However, many soldiers felt the same way he did; they couldn't stand the thought of leaving their families behind. They were beaten down and felt trapped in a hopeless situation that seemed to have no end in sight. It had begun for them as exiled prisoners; and now they were soldiers with another type of confinement and loss of freedom.

In a few minutes the lieutenant returned.

"All of those soldiers whose wives, children, old mothers, and other dependents are still here, please step forward."

At least 52 soldiers of various ranks in the battalion stepped forward.

"You will all be allowed to leave in a later transport after you have made arrangements to bring your families with you. Now, step back into formation."

After they were dismissed, crowds of men surrounded Tadeusz, thanking him profusely. He was the hero of the day. The soldiers told him how their family members were sick and how concerned they all were. They thanked him with tears in their eyes. They were overwhelmed with the enormity of what had just happened. So many families had already disappeared and, yet, they would stay together with theirs! This simple event was monumental in their lives.

Colonel Rezinski never forgot the outspoken soldier. Many years later, in a chance meeting in Barbara, Palestine, Colonel Rezinski recognized Tadeusz. He made it a point to thank him for changing the fate of so many people. At the time when the colonel gave his orders, he had not known that the Polish General Anders had already decided to keep the families together. No one, not even Churchill, was going to dissuade Anders from that decision. He knew how important it was for the families to stay together. He himself had spent years in a Siberian prison camp.

When Polish Army troops arrived in Persia, the British were surprised at the number of civilians who accompanied the soldiers. They had only planned on the soldiers; they had not realized that the Poles were escaping Russian slavery, and that the soldiers would not abandon their families in Uzbek. A Foreign Office minute to Churchill (dated March 31, 1942) from the Ambassador in Teheran stated that although they would have to put up between 10,000 to 15,000 civilians, they would be getting nearly 86,000 Polish troops out of Russia.[5] The British soon realized that if the troops were forced to leave their families, their morale would not be good. Churchill was not pleased that so many civilians were tagging along, but General Anders ignored his displeasure.

It was shortly after Taduesz's day of being a hero that he was given a pass to visit his wife in the hospital. His joy was indescribable because Helena's fever broke that day—she would live! She was extremely glad to see him, but also embarrassed when her hair began falling out as a result of the intense fever from typhus. Helena would wipe her hand over her head and it would be filled with clumps of hair that had come out at the roots. But, she was lucky because she lived.

Many friends and acquaintances were not so lucky. Among those who died was Kwiatkowski—the man who defended Tadeusz on the train. Because of Kwiatkowski's unsolicited words of admiration and praise for Tadeusz's unselfish acts of kindness, Tadeusz would never forget

---

5 Sword, K. (1994, p. 219, Note # 33). PRO PREM 3.354/1 Minute from Churchill attached to Ambassador Sir Reader Bullard's telegram.

him. Therefore, when Kwiatkowski's widow was designated to be left behind in Uzbek (since her soldier husband had died), Tadeusz came to her aid. Because she was no longer connected to the army, the army no longer had the responsibility for paying for her passage out of Russian territories. Tadeusz told the officials that she was his mother-in-law and that she was to leave with them. The story worked, and she left with them when the troops moved out. He probably saved her life, and he was glad to have been given the opportunity to repay a good deed.

ᕗ 19 ᕘ

Stationed in Persia

. . . Circumstances will dictate your choices.

At the end of August, Helena was scheduled to depart with other families heading for Iran. She would be joining Tadeusz, whose military transport had just left Krasnovodsk for Iran. Soviet military authorities ordered all the Poles to reduce their baggage to 44 pounds. Official Uzbek policy stated that they were to leave all their excess food and supplies in Uzbek S.S.R. They were also not allowed to take any Soviet rubles with them. One man defied the order to drop his money into a pile of rubles that was being accumulated by the guards. Instead, he set fire to all of his excess baggage and put the money on top of the burning pile. Immediately, a couple of Uzbek guards grabbed him and threatened to jail him. Other guards were telling the Poles not to take anything to eat with them since they were to be fed by the British. Helena disregarded the threats of the guards and was able to smuggle one tin of meat into her suitcase.

Helena had not been feeling well. It was only a short while ago that she had been ill with typhus, but now she knew that she coming down with a bout of malaria . . .

she had all the symptoms. Helena knew that she had to get on the boat, which was to cross the Caspian Sea from Krasnovodsk to Pahlevi, Persia. If she didn't get on it, she'd never see her husband again. So she found a soldier who was willing to sell her some quinine and she joined the rest of the families. They had to walk all evening to where the boat was waiting for them—7 km away. Other people noticed there was something wrong with her because her high fever was making her walk strangely. When an overly curious person began questioning her, saying that she shouldn't be with them if she was sick, another woman (a complete stranger) defended her. She told them that she and Helena had just split a bottle of wine and Helena was just reacting badly to the strong drink. Helena thanked God and asked Him to bless the woman for her good deed.

On the boat crossing the Caspian Sea, which was a 400-mile journey, she exchanged the tin of meat for a container of water. Unfortunately the man who exchanged the water for the meat was robbed. He then tried to insist that since he no longer had the meat, she should give back the water. He even tried to accuse her of stealing the meat. However, too many people saw that she never left her bunk once she lay down. The man had no reason to accuse her or to take away the water. Despite the harassment, she considered herself lucky. There was one woman traveling with two children who was accused of stealing food. They tried to frighten her into admitting to the theft, saying that they would get the soldiers to ship her back to Russia. Whether or not she took the food to feed her children, they should not have frightened her. The poor woman collapsed from a heart attack and died, leaving the two children orphaned.

When Helena arrived in Pahlevi, Persia, it was already September 14, 1942; two years and seven months since she had been deported from her home in Poland. She had lived a lifetime in less than three years. When she arrived, she was sent to a large tented campsite (number 6) near Teheran. There, her health somewhat improved after she got over her initial bout of fever. However, malaria doesn't just go away. It keeps reoccurring periodically throughout the years causing fever, chills, and memory loss. Malaria ended up killing many of the exiled Poles—perhaps not as many as typhus did, but it was still a serious disease.

After some months, life in Iran/Persia began to normalize for the Polish refugees. They took jobs in different trades, opened shops, started up theaters, and sold homemade goods. Some were employed in the hospitals, others in restaurants and bakeries. At first the Polish exiles disturbed the Iranians with their foreign customs and (probably) the competition for jobs. Eventually, however, the Iranians welcomed the Polish presence—perhaps only because of the propaganda they could promote. Not only would Iran appear more generous and hospitable than the Soviet Union, but the presence of starving Poles newly arrived from Russia indicated the sorry state of affairs in that country.[6] They couldn't resist poking fun at their Russian neighbors. Regardless of the reason, the Poles brought a new vitality to the Iranian community.

While Tadeusz was in training and quartered in the military barracks in Pahlevi, Helena was quartered with other civilians in the Teheran area. Her supplies were low so she decided to go into town to purchase a few items. She

---

6 Sword, K. (1994, p. 219, Note #47). PRO FO371/32627 W5303. Telegram no. 444 (Teheran to Foreign Office), 7 April 1942.

needed a suitcase and needles and thread to mend their clothing. They had been using cloth sacks to carry their possessions, so they needed something more substantial.

Helena and a girlfriend named Ryniewicz walked the short distance to the underground bazaars of Teheran. The underground tunnels were all dark—lit by lamplight and occasional grates in the ceiling that let in daylight. The sounds, smells, and colors were excitingly foreign to them. They were so interested in the strange exotic surroundings that they lost track of time. When they finally got out of the bazaars, evening had set in. To add to their misfortune, they had lost their bearings completely. Worse yet, they didn't know the name of the street that led to the camp. They hadn't been in Iran long enough to become familiar with Teheran. Ryniewicz began to panic. She had a timid nature and reacted with fright to the smallest thing. Soon, she became a nuisance with her hysterical reactions to every shadow and sound.

Helena asked a man in a restaurant for directions to Camp 6, but he was of no use. Another man led them in the wrong direction so that they had to return back to town. Finally, they came across a Polish priest. They recognized that he was a priest by his clothing. Unfortunately their happiness was quickly dashed. Instead of listening to the two ladies as they tried to ask for directions, he started cursing at them. He called them whores who were looking for action in the streets. Why else, he insisted, would two unaccompanied women be walking around at night? Helena was flabbergasted. With anger and disgust in her voice, she ripped into him.

"Exactly what are *you* doing out here at this time of night? It can't be to do the Lord's work. Obviously, given the strong reaction you're having to the sight of two lost women, you must be regretting the fact that you're supposed to be celibate. How dare you call us harlots instead of helping us find our way home! We saw a fellow countryman and thought we'd finally get some directions. Instead, we get the devil in the disguise of a priest. You're an evil man!"

They tried heading in yet another direction. Fortunately, they finally came upon an English soldier driving a jeep. He gave them directions to their camp and they finally made it back safely.

It seems that shopping expeditions into town always turned out to be an adventure. In another incident, Helena and two other women decided to go shopping in Teheran. They walked to the town, made their purchases, and then headed back to camp. One of the women suggested that they hitchhike. Helena and the other woman thought it was a bad idea until the first woman said she always hitchhiked and nothing ever happened.

A taxi cab driver stopped for them, they got in, and he started driving toward the camp. The lady who had supposedly hitchhiked before sat in front with the driver, while Helena and the other woman sat in back. Suddenly, the driver turned completely around and headed back to town. The women screamed as they realized what was happening. They were being kidnapped! Helena and the passenger in the back seat jumped out of the moving taxi. The driver grabbed the remaining lady's arm, detaining her as best he could. She struggled and beat at him until he released his hold on her. Then she also jumped out of the moving cab.

Everyone made sure that the women in the camps were informed about the dangers of hitchhiking with the

Women's Auxiliary Services Garrison Company; General Anders
(center) and Helena (standing seventh from left)

locals after that. It was a lesson well learned. They had
been lucky. Unfortunately, many women were kidnapped
and used in the brothels of Iran. They brought in a good
price for slavers because they were Caucasian, blond-
haired women . . . a rarity in the desert.

Helena officially joined the Polish Army on May 12,
1943, and she was reunited with Tadeusz who had not
been allowed to stay with her in her civilian encampment. At this point, 74,000 Polish troops were composed
of volunteers rescued from Soviet Russia. They were
armed and trained and were preparing to take part in
the Italian campaign. Some troops were already in Iraq
and Palestine (Israel did not yet exist), while others were
getting ready to depart for Egypt. Now that both Helena and Tadeusz were in the service, there would be more
opportunities for them to earn money and still be able to
stay together. Helena wanted to serve in communications

as a secretary. She requested office and typing training. Instead, they assigned her to guard duty.

One of her assignments was to police a camp that was 3 km from the outskirts of Teheran. During that assignment, she managed to catch a thief stealing a local merchant's rugs. However, she was glad that she never had to discharge her weapon at any time while performing guard duty. Having to kill or injure another person because of a stolen rug was not the kind of military service she had signed up for.

Helena remained in Iran for a short time after Tadeusz was sent to Iraq before she was also stationed there. She was assigned to the Polish Women's Auxiliary Services Garrison Company in Baghdad on June 3, 1943. Tadeusz was stationed 300 km away and as a result, it was nearly impossible for him to visit. Passes for travel around Iraq were suspended because too many men were frequenting brothels and causing trouble in local towns. The soldiers' unruly behavior offended the moral codes of the Muslims. It was also becoming too dangerous to travel. Marauding Arabs (with anti-British sentiments) were waylaying soldiers; murder was a constant occurrence.

Although Tadeusz was unable to get military passes for travel within Iraq, he was determined to see his wife. It was difficult for him to be separated from the only person who meant anything to him. Helena had had another bout with malaria in Iraq, and he was worried about her welfare. Therefore, he continued to visit her whenever he could . . . naturally, without a pass. Tadeusz would hitchhike on army trucks and sometimes travel by train. That was a little harder to do, and it required clever and evasive tactics. If some train conductor, or an official passed by, he pretended to be sleeping. If someone was checking documents, he'd ride on the outside of the train. He did whatever he had to do just to see her.

Tadeusz usually had phenomenal luck and was able to get away with his unauthorized travels. Once, however, he was not so fortunate and was detained by some British troops. The guards made the mistake of putting him into a tent while they were checking their records. One guard had been posted at the entrance; so, with that exit blocked, Tadeusz picked up the back flap of the tent and took off like a bullet. He was lucky and he knew it. It wasn't that easy to travel without a pass.

☞ 20 ☜

Palestine and Italy

. . . You will go through the cataclysm physically unscathed.

After their tour of duty in Iraq, both of the Szelazeks were eventually sent to Palestine for training. Once there, Tadeusz was stationed in Julius, not far from the Gaza Strip. He was in a camp, some distance away from Helena, when she was admitted into the hospital in Rehovot with yet another bout of malaria. Tadeusz visited her there (without a pass) and decided to hitchhike back by military transport.

This particular vehicle had a canvas tarp stretched across a metal framework, which covered the truck. It was filled to capacity with soldiers who were just coming off leave. They were singing and rocking the truck till it swayed dangerously back and forth. The driver was also driving a bit too fast for the road conditions. This road, near Gedera, was fairly treacherous; it was narrow and twisting, with deep cliffs and ravines alongside it. The recklessness of the driver made Tadeusz very nervous, so he tapped on the window of the cab.

"Hey, buddy, aren't you driving too fast? You're all behaving a bit dangerously."

The drunken soldiers on the truck started hooting, and putting him down.

"There's a chicken aboard. Stop the truck. Throw him off."

"Okay, if this is what you all want and it doesn't bother you, it doesn't bother me."

Ignoring the catcalls, he gave up trying to get them to behave more safely. He was fighting a little bit of a cold; so he covered himself with a blanket and curled up inside a large spare tire that rested against the cab of the truck. He took a few sips of some Wisniowka (cherry liquor) and fell asleep. The next thing he knew, he felt a tremendous impact; his eyes flew open, and then everything went dark.

"This is it, I must be dead. I can't move, I can't breathe. I have to pray."

When he heard the moans; he realized that he was covered with the bodies of the other passengers. He pushed the bodies off and found that the truck had fallen off a bridge and into a deep ravine. Most of the people had died upon impact, just because of the sheer height of the fall. Others were pierced through their bodies with the shattered metal bars of the truck's framework; they acted like spears. Nineteen soldiers were dead, and the others were all critically injured. Tadeusz sustained a little scratch and a slightly ripped shirt. The large tire had saved his life by providing cushioning and armor against the metal rods.

Rescue parties eventually climbed down the cliffs with ropes and began to lift out the bodies. Tadeusz couldn't let anyone know he was traveling without a pass, so, as soon as he could disengage himself from the mass of bodies, he pretended to be a part of the rescue team. When the opportunity presented itself, he climbed up the side of the ravine and slipped away unnoticed in all of the commotion. He hitched a ride further down the road and made it back to his company without being caught.

An hour after he had left her, Helena heard about the accident. She had an overwhelming feeling that something was dreadfully wrong with Tadeusz. The area where the truck had fallen off a cliff, in Gedera, was known for having a number of accidents occur weekly. She promptly enlisted the help of another patient to cover up for her absence from the hospital. If questioned about Helena's whereabouts, she was to tell the nurse that Helena was in the hospital entertainment room watching a movie. Quickly, she hitchhiked to the accident site. When she saw the wreck, she hoped that the smashed truck had not been carrying Tadeusz; although, for some reason, she felt this was the same one.

When she arrived, the majority of the truck's occupants were already dead and of those soldiers who were alive, most were seriously injured. A few were asking to be killed so they could be released from their agony. One man, whose legs had been cut off, clutched at Helena, begging her to help him end his life. He didn't wish to live without his legs. She gave him water and encouraged him to fight for his life.

After not finding Tadeusz among the dead or injured, she assumed he had either been on another truck or had escaped the accident uninjured. It was morning by the time she hitchhiked back to the hospital. She asked the English officer who gave her a ride back to stop some distance from the building. Obviously, he knew she was AWOL from the hospital, but he didn't try to stop her. She snuck into the chapel and from there into the hospital. Fortunately for Helena, the patient (to whom Helena had spoken the evening before) helped cover for her. She had told the nurse, who was taking morning temperatures that Helena was in the chapel praying. Then, when Helena was actually seen walking from the chapel, the story was substantiated. The next day, all her worries were alleviated when Tadeusz sent a message saying that he was all right despite having been in the accident.

∽

Some time after this incident, Helena found she was pregnant again. She awaited the new child with hopefulness and concern. Maybe she was finally going to have the child they had been longing for. In her fifth month of pregnancy, in March of 1944, she was assigned to the army's Expectant Mothers' Home (for dependents and female soldiers). She was a little downhearted because Tadeusz had already been sent with the Third Division Carpathian Infantry to Italy that January. He would not be back before the baby was to be born. The Expectant Mothers' Home in Ram Allah, Palestine (now Jordan), had 60 women in residence at the time. Pregnant soldiers were still not very common, and spare, larger-sized uniforms were unavailable. Purchasing new uniforms was financially impossible for most of the soldiers, even if there had been some available. So, all the ladies had to wear their regular uniforms to full term. There were many seams and insets that had to be let out before this feat could be accomplished. The women in this group formed fast friendships; all were separated from their husbands, and all were alone while they were giving birth. Helena missed her husband dreadfully and wrote letters to him constantly. She wished he could be a part of this important time in their lives. The letters she received from him didn't take his place, but they did help relieve some of her worry about him.

Meanwhile, Tadeusz and his company were stationed in Italy where they encountered German resistance in places like Capracotta, San Pietro, Faenza, Senigallia, Loreto, Osimo, Ancona, Bryzgiella, Canossa, Taranto, Apenina, Adriatic, Pescara, Rimini, Pesaro, and Bologna. The horrors of war stood in stark contrast to the beautiful landscape of this country. Everywhere he looked, war was destroying irreplaceable buildings, works of art, and, most importantly, lives. War was all senseless brutality . . . brutality that was sometimes mirrored in some of the soldiers' acts. Ignorant, uneducated soldiers practiced shooting at targets using priceless marble statuary, or they ransacked villas with irreplaceable artwork. This handful of misguided individuals justified everything they did by saying that they were only punishing the Fascists. Tadeusz tried to reason with them whenever he witnessed these rampages, but to his disgust, they rarely listened. Stronger disciplinary actions by concerned officers eventually curbed these atrocities.

Tadeusz's intelligence, abilities, and outrageous humor were soon recognized by those around him. Soldiers flocked to his side for advice, friendship, and entertainment. People loved to socialize with him. He would often have high-ranking officers step into his tent for a chat or a drink after duty. Among his guests was Wladyslaw Anders, the commander of the Polish forces—the same General for whom Roman, Tadeusz's brother, had worked as personal secretary. Another guest was Bronislawa (Szabatowska) Wyslouchowa, a colonel in the Polish Army under British command. Colonel Wyslouchowa

Rohovot, Palestine

was in charge of all the female soldiers in General Anders'
command. Tadeusz had become acquainted with her and
her husband before the war. They met during a business
trip when Tadeusz still owned a Spolem franchise in

Poland. Colonel Wyslouchowa's husband, unfortunately, had died in 1937, leaving her a young widow. At that time, she had been a newspaper editor and courageously became a part of the Polish Resistance until 1941, when she was captured, tortured, sentenced to death, and sent to prison to wait for her sentence to be carried out. After the amnesty, General Anders personally interceded on her behalf and secured her release from prison. She subsequently enlisted in the army and was one of the thousands of female soldiers who worked alongside their male counterparts in the Women's Auxiliary Army. It was in Iran/Persia that females were finally given credit for their work and were recognized as full-fledged soldiers. They were allowed to become officers in the Polish Army under British command. They were put in charge of transportation, communication, food preparation, medical care, intelligence, supplies, and security, among other duties.

Now, while stationed in Italy with their troops waging battle at Monte Cassino, Colonel Wyslouchowa met up with Tadeusz again. She had been quartered in the officer's campsite in Ancona, and one night while Tadeusz was visiting her for one of their occasional evening chats, General Anders dropped in. Tadeusz immediately sprang into a formal salute, but Anders insisted that he drop the formality.

"No, my friend, you don't have to salute."

He repeated the request twice. Then he added, "You were here before I was, and it is I who am intruding here. If Miss Bronislawa wishes, she could take me by the collar and toss me out of the door. Please, sit down, join us."

Bronislawa brought out a bottle of Vermouth and poured some drinks. The ensuing conversation was pleasant and witty. She was an intelligent, gracious woman whose presence brought civility, even onto the battlefield.

It was not long afterward that Tadeusz had another chance meeting with the general. Tadeusz was visiting with a friend from Dywin—Lieutenant Arciszewski. As a civilian, the lieutenant had been a teacher, but now he was working in Army Intelligence. Tadeusz was sitting with his back to the tent door when General Anders entered.

"I see you have a guest, so I'll come back later when you're free."

"General, sir, this is my best friend from Dywin, Private Tadeusz Szelazek. You can talk freely in front of him."

Tadeusz snapped a salute to the general.

"Oh, it's you, my good friend! No matter where I look, you seem to be there."

The general continued his business with the lieutenant and left. Later on, Arciszewski asked Tadeusz, "How in the world do you know the general? He said you were a fascinating person and he called you his friend."

But, in fact, it was Tadeusz's friendships with people of all rank, such as Colonel Bronislawa Wyslouchowa, or Lieutenant Arciszewski, or even General Anders, that often worked against him. Tadeusz's popularity apparently caused a couple of his superior officers to have fits of jealousy. They could not compete with his popularity, courage, and leadership qualities. More often than not, the soldiers in Tadeusz's platoon would follow his lead during a crisis. It was rumored that "Szelazek had nine lives like a cat," so he was the one to keep close to in battle. Tadeusz never opposed or disobeyed any orders; but he made lightning speed decisions and assessed life-threatening situations so quickly, that he reacted before others even had a chance to think about it. The other soldiers instinctively followed his lead without debate or hesitation.

Tadeusz's popularity and leadership qualities especially infuriated a certain Captain Nowak and the captain's friend, Lieutenant Krysiak. They were determined to find something they could use against him. If they could discredit him to the other soldiers or possibly get him court-martialed, they would get even with the "civilian" upstart. Tadeusz did not care for military life and preferred the civilian life, wearing regular clothing whenever it was allowed. They implemented their plan by first intercepting all his mail. They opened each letter and reviewed its content. They hoped Helena might bring up something embarrassing, or perhaps a letter from him would disclose secret information, complaints, or scandalous materials. There was nothing. Helena would usually write about her work in Palestine and the loneliness she felt without him. But mostly, she kept her letters positive and amusing, knowing how difficult it was for him to be in the middle of a war zone.

Helena began to notice that some of his letters looked as if they had been opened and then resealed. There were also gaps in their correspondence as though he didn't get certain letters from her. Therefore, some of her questions to him remained unanswered. In coded language she indicated that perhaps someone was reviewing their mail. Tadeusz had developed a way of communicating with Helena in a language that had double meanings and therefore was almost cryptic. They began corresponding in this sort of fashion while he started an investigation. He found out from the soldier assigned to mail delivery that one of the sergeants personally took all of the mail addressed to Tadeusz (or written by Tadeusz) and delivered it to Captain Nowak. Armed with this information, Tadeusz reported this mail tampering to a certain lieutenant friend of his, who had the quarters of both Lieutenant Krysiak and Captain Nowak searched. They found 23 letters that belonged to Tadeusz in the captain's quarters!

Faced with an imminent court-martial for tampering with mail for personal reasons, Captain Nowak sent a messenger to summon Tadeusz to his quarters for a "conversation." The messenger arrived while Tadeusz was in his tent talking with some of his buddies.

"Is the Captain asking me to see him, or ordering me to see him? I am off duty at the moment and, therefore, you should ask him if this is official business or not."

This took the messenger completely by surprise, and he left to get a specific explanation as to whether this message was an order or request from the captain. His departure was followed by hoots of laughter from the other men in the tent. They especially enjoyed the unusual situation and the verbal jousting that had just occurred. Their captain was a crude, uncultured, sadistic officer, and few people would pity him if he were court-martialed. The messenger came back.

"The Captain asked whether you would be available for a private conversation."

"Tell him I will be available in an hour. I have some tasks to attend to first."

Tadeusz arrived after an hour's delay. He was admitted into the tent and was asked to sit down. The captain began with a noncommittal apology, not actually admitting any wrongdoing.

"I want to apologize. Please don't be angry with me."

"I'm not angry with anyone. I never am. I'm just worried that you will be angry with me with the upcoming court-martial."

Captain Nowak began suggesting that perhaps there was something he could do, perhaps get or arrange something for him. Anything, just so he could change Tadeusz's mind about pressing charges.

"No, I don't need, want, or require anything. We are all in the same war together. We all have the same needs and we are all judged by the same God. So, if we're finished with our conversation, I will be taking my leave. Good night, Captain Nowak."

Tadeusz later heard that Nowak was worried that somehow Tadeusz was going to get revenge on him in the field; or perhaps Nowak would meet God prematurely. There was no need for him to worry on that account. Justice was served with the court-martial.

⤏ 21 ⤎

A Baby Is Born

You will have . . . three daughters.

Back in Palestine, Helena started going into labor on a Saturday night, but none of the Hebrew doctors were available to assist her at the Expectant Mothers' Home. She gave birth without the aid of a doctor, but it was not an easy birth. No one with the medical knowledge necessary to give her an episiotomy had been present, so she had subsequently suffered vaginal tearing. A doctor finally arrived seven hours later to look in on her, but because of the lack of medical supplies, new complications arose. Her internal tears had not been sutured closed, and they also did not have sterile gauze available for her. With all the bleeding and torn skin, she soon developed an infection. She was forced to deal with this serious health issue as she tried to care for her newborn.

Her daughter, Krystyna, was born in July of 1944 in Jaffa, Palestine. She was a gorgeous dark-haired, chubby-cheeked girl. Helena feared letting her child out of her sight, but she was in too much pain to care for all Krystyna's needs. She allowed the nurses at the home to care for her child. Unfortunately, one of the nurses, named Lurowa, put too much disinfectant into the bath water and she blistered Krystyna's delicate skin. Another baby was also seriously injured in this incompetent care-giving. This was almost too much for Helena to bear. She was fighting both pain and fear for her daughter's life. Two of her children were already dead and now her third newborn was injured almost as soon as she was born. An army doctor advised her to puncture the blisters which covered the baby's body, squeeze out the fluid, and put an iodine-based compound on the ruptured skin. While Krystyna cried out with the pain, Helena cried along with her.

A few days later, Helena was able to take her baby to the doctors at the Hebrew Hadassah hospital. There, she was told not to worry because Krystyna was healing and her skin would be fine. This greatly relieved Helena's overwhelming anxiety. The doctors at the Hadassah had excellent reputations and were known for saving many lives.

Helena was honorably discharged from military service on December 31, 1944 in Ram Allah, Palestine. Although her enlistment had been short, she was later awarded the Defense Medal, The War Medal 1939–45, and The Polish Army Medal. She took great pride in being involved in the Middle East peacekeeping duties of the British. The people of Great Britain would always have a special place in her heart; actually, in all the Siberian deportees' hearts. They made it possible to escape the nightmares of exile in Russia.

☞ 22 ☜

Avoiding Bullets

. . . a hail of bullets . . . but none will touch you.

War gives people the opportunity to reflect upon the past, contemplate the future, and appreciate the present. Tadeusz had been in Italy for some time now. He hadn't thought about the old psychic's words for quite a while. Yet, now, he was beginning to think that perhaps he wasn't meant to die in this war after all. It seemed that many of the things that had been foretold to him were already coming or had come true. Tadeusz suspected that he was being saved for something special; although, just what that was, he had no clue. He had always taken chances before, but now he felt fearless, and his actions were almost foolhardy. He didn't consider what he did as "acts of bravery" since he knew he wasn't meant to die. Tadeusz routinely volunteered for dangerous assignments, rushing out to save his comrades when they were down.

In one incident, his company was pinned down on a rock-strewn hillside. The hot sun was blazing down upon the parched men who were totally out of water. The large containers in which the water had been kept were accidentally contaminated with gasoline. Now there was nothing for them to drink and the heat was creating agony. However, a short distance away from them stood a well in the middle of a field. No one wanted to risk his life to venture out for water, however. There was no cover, which made it a perfect place to get hit by sniper fire. So, Tadeusz collected as many of the men's canteens as he could carry. Ignoring the warnings and protests from all of the other soldiers near him, he ran through the field right up to the well. Bullets buzzed by him like maddened hornets. Shards of rock and dirt hit him as the bullets ricocheted around him. He filled up all of the canteens, throwing away a couple of those that were damaged by bullet holes. Then he ran back, and distributed the canteens among the men around him. He took off his backpack and looked inside for some K-rations. The insides of the bag looked as if a rat had made a nest in it. He carefully unrolled a hunk of material that used to be a shirt and found a lead bullet all balled up inside of it. The contents of his knapsack had deflected the bullet which should have killed him.

Now it was official. He was the crazy Pole who had no fear. His superior officer, Lieutenant Krysiak, made his way over to the small company of men who were enjoying the cool, clean water from their canteens. When he found out that Tadeusz provided them with the water, he was enraged. It didn't help that he was still smarting from the backlash of Captain Nowak's court-martial (which had been precipitated by Tadeusz's complaint). If anyone else, other than Szelazek, had provided his company with water, he would have been grateful to the soldier and would have written him up for a medal. Instead, he cursed Tadeusz for being a foolhardy lunatic.

In another incident, their truck was traveling through enemy territory. They were moving slowly up a narrow road when Tadeusz noticed some movement in the bushes. Although the truck was still moving, Tadeusz jumped off the back, shouting to the others to beware of an ambush. He was shooting his Tommy gun before he even touched the ground. Somehow, this caught the German snipers off guard. Ordinarily, soldiers would wait until the trucks were completely stopped before they started shooting. The momentary hesitation cost the German soldiers their advantage. By the time they organized their response, everyone in Tadeusz's company was lobbing grenades and shooting up the terrain. The Poles won the skirmish that day. Again, Lieutenant Krysiak was furious with Tadeusz.

"I'm supposed to give the orders to shoot around here!"

"I didn't hear any orders being given."

"I am responsible for your life!"

"No, with all due respect, I am responsible for my life, which is in God's hands, not yours. If I were to commit suicide right now, on this spot, you could not prevent it nor would you be responsible for it either. Whether I live or I die is my choice."

There was nothing more to be said. Krysiak reprimanded him, saying he wasn't doing things by the book. He told Tadeusz that it was not his place to shout orders for the truck to stop or for the soldier to start shooting. That was Krysiak's job.

The other soldiers who crowded around them burst out laughing at the reprimand and that infuriated Krysiak even further. Tadeusz was far too fearless for his own good and was showing him up. What made things worse was that a war medal for military valor, the Wojenny Vertuti

Militari, was to be awarded by the Polish government to Tadeusz for his part in that very same skirmish, but Krysiak turned it down in Tadeusz's name, without informing him. (The Vertuti Militari is one of the oldest medal decorations still in use in the world today.) Krysiak's reasoning for refusing the medal in Tadeusz's name was that Tadeusz was no more responsible for the final outcome of that battle than any other individual in the company. Instead of getting angry, Tadeusz laughed at him.

"One medal is no better than another and I don't need medals to document my bravery, or anything else for that matter. They won't buy me a loaf of bread."

Then there was the incident in Osimo, Italy. Tadeusz accidentally got separated from his company and was making his way toward a village. He walked through some cornfields, past a house, and headed toward a barn on the outskirts of town. As he passed by the barn, an elderly Italian woman signaled to him.

"Sssh! Tedeski (Germans)!" She pointed to the second floor of the building nearby. He was able to make out the voices of two soldiers talking in German.

Tadeusz plastered himself against the wall, realizing that a company of Germans was quartered there. It dawned on him that he had passed the front lines and was well into enemy territory. Quickly, he ducked back into the cornfield, crawled through a hay field, belly-crawled across a stream, and finally headed up in the direction of a British division that was making its way toward him from that direction. The British tanks were on the road advancing toward the town. He ran up to one of the tanks, climbed on top on it, and started pounding on the cover. This was totally incorrect behavior. The poor British soldier inside was extremely shaken. The frightened soldier burst through the cover and pointed a gun at the insistent intruder. At first he thought he was being attacked, and then he saw the Polish uniform.

"You crazy Polak, I could have killed you!"

Tadeusz had picked up a little of the English language and did his best to communicate the danger that they were driving into. He pointed to the buildings in the distance.

"There, there, German soldiers, in village."

As he stood there, on the side of the tank, a spray of machine gun fire hit the surface. You could almost see an outline of his body on the tank, but none of the bullets touched him. It was like watching a cartoon silhouette appear on the metal side of the tank. The Englishman yelled at him to get to cover behind the tank; and then he aimed the tank's guns toward the source of the German gunfire. Tadeusz ducked behind the tank, headed for cover, and then checked himself for holes. He marveled at the fact that not only was he alive but also not even scratched. The tank commanders took careful aim, and after a few rounds, the buildings were all leveled. All Tadeusz could think about was the poor old woman who had warned him of the danger and prayed that she was safe from the destruction that was happening all around them.

⟨ 23 ⟩

War, Peace, and Relocation

There will be a Great War that will involve the whole world. . .

After the collapse of the Italian Fascist regime in 1943, German troops occupied the town of Cassino, Italy. More importantly, the Germans were occupying a monastery located on the hill called Monte Cassino. Its prominent, inaccessible location made it a fortress. Obviously, it was vital that the Allies occupy that hill since it overlooked the main road to Rome. They had to take control of the monastery at any cost. The Allied troops would be unable to pass this point safely unless the Germans were rousted.

The resulting battle of Monte Cassino was an indescribable inferno. Most of the action occurred at night, as the armies of different nations tried to scale the sides of the mountain. First, the Americans failed to gain control of the hill; they were followed by the troops from India and New Zealand. They also failed. Then the Poles asked permission to advance against the Germans on the hill. They were led by one of their own, General Anders.

The Polish soldiers were making a name for themselves in this war. They were being sent wherever there was an involvement with the Germans. They had even earned the name of Desert Rats from the Germans they had fought. Then, in Italy, Anders saw the opportunity for the world to focus their attention on the plight of the Poles.

It had taken Anders only ten minutes to decide on the Poles' involvement in the battle of Monte Cassino. He wanted the world to know that even though the Poles no longer had a homeland; they would fight for the freedom of any country that stood against the Germans. The Poles had to show the world that they were a brave, independent people who would not allow any country, including the Russians, to hold them as prisoners. This battle was a battle for freedom on all levels.

The Poles had 28 days to prepare for the battle. They used nets to camouflage their activities along the road to Monte Cassino. Covered wagons carried the ammunition, which was then, in turn, passed on to smaller vehicles, and then onto jeeps. As the road narrowed, the ammunition and supplies were transferred to and carried up by donkeys. Eventually, the road became a mere path up the side of the mountain. Then, even that path became so steep that donkeys were ineffective. Everything had to be carried up on the backs of the soldiers. They strung a ribbon to mark the best access to the top of the mountain.

Tadeusz hitched a ride in an ammo truck during one of the trips up the side of the mountain. All the other soldiers got off the truck as the driver prepared to complete the treacherous trip up alone. But Tadeusz told the driver that if it was safe enough for him to drive up this road, than it should be safe enough for Tadeusz to accompany him. Unfortunately, the truck slid down the side of the cliff and then rolled over several times before eventually hanging itself up on a huge tree. This was the fortunate part, since the ravine continued down for a long distance. Tadeusz managed to escape with only a bruised head—definitely a miracle since he wasn't even wearing a helmet.

His friends had a good laugh at his latest escapade. "Szelazek is like a cat. You throw him down a cliff and he lands on his feet. It was sure lucky for the driver that Tadeusz decided to tag along with him."

Fortunately the driver of the truck was uninjured although the supplies were spread across the side of the ravine.

The Polish army's attack on the monastery began at 11:00 p.m. on May 11, 1944. The code word was "Honkers" for the sound of wild geese flying home. At first, there was dead silence; then two hours of brutal shelling and bombing began. Toward dawn, the attack ended and the Poles had achieved a position near the base of the monastery. Many dead and injured soldiers had fallen in areas totally exposed to shelling and sniper fire. Their bodies could not be retrieved in broad daylight without endangering the lives of the rescuers. So, as the heat of the sun beat down on the helpless, injured soldiers, attempts to rescue them ceased till evening fell.

Tadeusz fought without a care for his own safety. He would urge others onward because he knew that his fate (and his fellow soldiers' fate) was in the hands of God. Sometimes he would look back, just in time to see the area he had left, blow up. Often, other soldiers who had been too slow, or unwilling to move forward, never left again. At one point in the battle, when he had been fighting for three days without sleep, he positioned himself by a large rock in an area that he was ordered to secure. The shelling was tapering off and the evening would soon arrive. Suddenly appearing out of nowhere, Tadeusz's mother was standing next to him.

This was impossible! How could this be? She was in Poland, wasn't she?

"Mamma, what are you doing here?"

"You can't stand here, move away from here. Now!"

"But I can't. I've been told to stay in this area."

"Then, if you have to stay . . . please, move over there."

She pointed to an area and started moving away from where Tadeusz was standing. He followed her and when he reached the spot she had indicated, she started to fade away. He called for her but she disappeared completely. He knew something was wrong. Something out of the ordinary had just happened. But what did it mean? Was his mother, who he knew was back at home in Poland, dead? Was he hallucinating from lack of sleep?

He closed his eyes and prayed for her, and then he prayed for his wife and the child he had not yet seen. Then, he prayed for himself. Before he knew it, he fell asleep. When he awoke he felt something lying on top of him, as if he was buried alive. Blood was flowing from his ears and nose. He pushed away the dirt and surveyed his surroundings. He had fallen asleep inside a shallow depression in the ground. He looked at the place he was standing earlier that evening. The debris, that was now covering him, was all that remained of the large rock. It was blown to bits by a mortar shell.

Many months later, Tadeusz found out that his mother was still alive in Poland. She had been constantly praying for him. It seems that God had allowed her to warn him in this strange fashion.

The second attack on the Monastery began on May 18 at 5:00 a.m. The Poles had their victory by 10:20 a.m.

But, it was a victory that cost the Polish soldiers dearly . . . over 1,000 were dead and 2,000 were wounded. The wounded were treated by Polish doctors who, with the aid of the Red Cross from America, used penicillin for the first time to treat infections. As for the dead, the Polish soldiers built a cemetery directly upon the spot where their countrymen perished. They had no free homeland to ship their comrades to; so their fallen comrades' homes were now a plot of land at Monte Cassino. At the base of the cemetery is an inscription in Polish: "Passerby, tell Poland that we fell faithfully in her service, for our freedom and yours. We Polish soldiers gave our souls to God, our bodies to the soil of Italy, and our hearts to Poland." A song was written to commemorate the slaughter at Monte Cassino with a verse stating, "The poppies on Monte Cassino will be a brighter red because of the blood of Poles."

This was not the only place where more Polish blood was being spilled. Because they lacked a free Poland to return to, the Polish government-in-exile was located in England. Poland still belonged to the Russian communists and the exiles had had enough of the Russians. Their families and friends back in Poland were still suffering at their hands. They would not return to their homeland until it was free of Russian rule. However, on August 1, 1944, the Russians made it perfectly clear that there would be a Russian government in Poland.

The Poles living in occupied Poland had staged the Warsaw Uprising on August 1, 1944, on orders of the Polish government-in-exile. They asked divisional General, Bor-Komorowski, to lead the resistance with the hope that the Russian Army would aid them in their battle against the Germans. The fighting lasted for 63 days while the Russians camped 20 km away, and refused to give assistance. They knew that if they waited it out, the Polish Resistance would be crushed. Stalin was not about to help the Poles with their "criminal adventure," which could prevent his complete takeover of Poland. The Poles, lead by Komorowski, had to surrender once they realized that the Russians were betraying them and the Polish Resistance fighters failed to hold the city. Then, with the Resistance scattered, the Russian Army walked in and claimed Warsaw as its own victory against the Germans.

Meanwhile, the battles in Italy were finally over. Tadeusz was given a pass (in March of 1945) to go to Egypt for some much needed rest and relaxation. However, once he arrived in Egypt, he was instructed (along with some of the other soldiers freshly arrived from Italy) to load and haul stones. Instead of giving him a leave, they put him on a work detail. He went into a rage at the injustice. He was a soldier and not a slave! Tadeusz insisted that he be allowed to see his wife in Palestine. They took what he said under consideration and, shortly thereafter, allowed him and the other Polish soldiers to go on leave. He finally saw his daughter Krystyna for the first time. She was already eight months old and was shy with the stranger who hugged and kissed her mother. Krystyna tried to push this strange man away from her mother but eventually made peace with him. After an all-too-brief visit, Tadeusz was sent back to Italy to finish with the clean-up.

After the Italian campaign was over, Tadeusz returned to Palestine in the summer of 1946. Krystyna was nearly two years old. The country was in a state of turmoil and unrest with Arab and Jewish factions warring constantly. Everyone was in constant danger and Helena began feeling more vulnerable than usual when she discovered that she was pregnant soon after Tadeusz's return. Although Tadeusz was then stationed in Barbara, Palestine, he was housed in the barracks of a nearby army camp. Helena, however, had already been discharged from the army and was living in a small, private complex of stucco-covered buildings. These buildings were connected with a common courtyard between them. There were no window-panes, only shutters in the walls, which could be closed against bad weather. Tadeusz was not able to visit her very often; so Helena found herself without his protection while Arab dissidents were attacking all the houses in the area. The terrorists had managed to rob and kill a number of soldiers and their families in the outlying regions. Their aims were specific. They were protesting the Jewish control of land that they had always considered their own. This constantly renewed fighting was as old as the Bible—never to be healed, never to be resolved.

One evening, the Arabs attacked the first house closest to the street. Helena quickly bolted the window shutters as the bullets started to hit her building. She laid Krystyna on the floor and covered her with pillows to stop any stray bullets. She had had to return her weapon when she was discharged from active military service, so she had no weapon to protect herself with. Fortunately, another family (by the name of Kaczorowski) lived in the same building. They helped hold off the Arab attack until help arrived. Mr. Kaczorowski barricaded the door and held it closed against the battering it was receiving from the outside. The owner of the complex got out onto the roof and started shooting at the marauders. He finally managed to scare them off. He was an Arab himself and was disgusted with the behavior of his own people who had acted like terrorists with no regard for innocent lives.

Summer 1946, Israel—after the Italian campaign ended

Tadeusz and Kaczorowski were both at the housing complex the next time that there was an attack in the area. They spent the night on the roof firing their weapons to discourage the Arabs from returning. After the terrorist attacks, the army allowed the families of the Polish soldiers to move into the army camps for protection. This was a wise move because, at that point, the camps were being attacked as well. During this time, the Szelazeks formed a fast bond of friendship with the Kaczorowski family, which they maintained through the following years.

Time was flying by and Krystyna was now a healthy, intelligent two-year-old. And, like every two-year-old, she knew her mind exactly. Her likes and dislikes were voiced emphatically. She told her mother that she wanted to have a brother. Krystyna had fallen in love with the neighbor's baby boy, and she kept telling her pregnant mom to be sure that the new baby was a boy. When the first pains came early, Helena and Tadeusz drove to the hospital. The doctor examined her but told her it would be weeks before she would deliver. The premature labor pains soon subsided and they drove back home. Tadeusz stopped by the toy store to pick up a doll for Krystyna. She was expecting them to return with a baby and he knew she would be disappointed. The gift was supposed to dull the disappointment.

Krystyna took one look at the doll and dashed it to the ground.

"This isn't a baby. I will kill this doll to death. I want a real boy."

She was ecstatic when her wish came true. A son, Jerzy (George), was born in Gilead, Tel Aviv, Palestine, on April 20, 1947. They called him Jureczek (little George). He was a beautiful baby with blue eyes and blond hair. His disposition was sweet and he was very gentle and loving. It was apparent from the start, however, that he had some sort of stomach defect. He appeared to be uncomfortable and colicky. He would cry and rub his cheek until the skin was rubbed red. The doctors at the Hadassah clinic gave him a special formula in the hopes that it would relieve some of his distress. Krystyna would spend hours patting his head gently and whispering to him to quiet him down. She would give him her favorite little red pillow to rest his head on. He was more than a brother to her and she constantly showed him her love.

The Szelazeks spent a total of four years in Palestine/ Israel; and they were still there when the war was finally over for the Polish exiles. The British government informed them that all of the soldiers, and their family members, were to be shipped out to England by way of Egypt. Poland was their homeland, but England was the next best thing. Very few families decided to go back to Poland for more abuse from the Russian Communists.

The Szelazeks packed their belongings and put their documents in order. They made provisions for the upcoming trip, and the most important item on their to-do list was to assess their financial state. Paper currency no longer had value as it had in the past and its value was even less outside of Palestine. Tadeusz used his paper currency to buy a few gold coins which he then used to make gold jewelry (of his design) for Helena. She finally had, for the first time in her life, something beautiful and valuable that she could hand down to her children. This small cache of gold jewelry, along with the picture of Christ that she always carried with them, were the only things of value left in their lives. Their ties with the past were broken. There was no free homeland to return to. So, what they carried was all they had in this world.

The new Israeli government forbade the removal of any money or gold from the country; so the Szelazeks had to find a way to transport their few pieces of jewelry safely. These pieces were the only security left to them against the possibility of total poverty. So, Tadeusz devised a plan to transport their small amount of gold jewelry. He

Helena in Ram Allah, Palestine (Jordan)

purchased a leather case and then unstitched the bottom of it. Money and jewelry were then inserted and the case was re-stitched. Helena then filled the case with diapers and baby bottles for Jureczek. They felt secure knowing that no one would want to steal a diaper bag. They encountered no trouble getting onto the boat that was taking them to their new lives in England.

Although many families were preparing to be shipped to Egypt, not all the families would be going. The families of deceased soldiers had to remain in the Middle East. These families were awarded a single pension check and then they were on their own in Palestine. This was an unfortunate decision on the part of the British government, because the Arabs eventually slaughtered most of the woman and children who were left in those abandoned camps.

The fate of many Poles was never determined after World War II. If the Polish Government estimates are accurate, then less than 10 percent of the Poles made it out of the Soviet territory in 1942. These were Poles who were deported from Eastern Poland by the Soviet authorities in the period between 1939 and 1941.[7] Incidents, like the Katyn Forest massacre, were common. This was where the bodies of some 4,000 Poles from the Kozielsk camp were found. Polish officers from the Starobielsk camps, as well as prisoners from the Ostashkov camps, were murdered there. With the decimation of Polish soldiers from disease, battles, and clashes with locals in the Middle East, the final number of survivors (from that 10 percent) was pathetically small.

---

7 Sword, K. (1994, p.vii).

❧ 24 ❧

Life in England, Loss, and Progress

. . . a great sorrow but . . . beyond your control . . .

Whooping Cough (Pertussis) was a common disease among the weak, overcrowded, starving mass of exiles. One of the families, on the boat heading for England, had a child infected with this disease. Ordinarily, they should have remained behind and had their child in quarantine, but they were afraid to be parted from the rest of the demobilized Polish Army. They were desperate to leave Palestine with the rest of their relatives. Unfortunately, the ill child spread the virus to 47 other children. (The bacteria spread by airborne droplets, affecting mostly infants and young children who are the least resistant.) Fortunately for the Szelazeks neither Krystyna nor Jureczek contracted the disease.

The weary family finally arrived in England in the summer of 1947. Helena was not looking forward to the complexities of going through customs in England. Tadeusz was following with the rest of the soldiers and was not there to help her out. She was worried about how she would keep the children safe, keep all their belongings in sight, and search for their luggage, all at the same time.

1947—Krystyna, Helena, Tadeusz, and Jurek

Helena decided to enlist the help of a British policeman who was standing duty at the docks. She asked him to help her with her logistical problem. She handed him the leather diaper case (which contained her jewelry) and baby Jureczek to hold for her. Then she took Krystyna with her to look for their suitcases. The policeman was a wonderful babysitter, and Helena returned to a scene of him cooing to a delighted gurgling infant.

The Szelazeks' first home was in the Families Camp Rivenhill in Witham, Essex. Their lodging left a lot to be desired by way of comfort; nevertheless, it was a home. They were labeled "displaced people" by the world, but finally they were living in a free country. The Russians, the terrorists, and the war were behind them and now they could finally settle down and create a home for themselves. Tadeusz was discharged from active service in the army on October 30, 1947, and was assigned to the Polish Resettlement Corps. (He received his final discharge papers from the Corps on September 30, 1949.)

Jureczek was now seven months old and a very active infant. He had safely made it through his exposure to whooping cough, but his stomach complaints continued. Some days he would be in obvious pain; and then, at other times, he would be an active normal child. One day, at the end of December 1947, he was crawling around vigorously when he suddenly started screaming with pain, holding his stomach. Helena rushed him down to the hospital where she was informed that the surgeon was going to operate on him immediately. The doctors began to explain Jureczek's condition. They called it *intussusception*. One section of the baby's intestines had begun to telescope in on itself. The condition could be compared to pulling a shirt sleeve partially inside out. The pain was intense and, if the problem were left untreated, the intestine would keep telescoping, cause blockages, infections, and death. Intussusception primarily occurs in infants and usually affects parts of the small intestine, or colon, when one section slides into another causing a blockage. The English doctors at that hospital had only seen one case in the past seven years. They recommended that the affected section of the intestine be cut out. The only problem was that the hospital's anesthesiologist didn't have any previous experience with this particular procedure. Because the baby was only seven months old, he wasn't sure how much anesthetic to give him. They told Helena they couldn't guarantee that he would survive the operation, but he definitely could not live with this serious condition.

The operation was a success, but the incorrect dosage of anesthetic put a strain on Jureczek. There may have also been other complications, but the end result was that his little body could not withstand the tremendous pain he was experiencing. He was dying. The nurse kept telling Helena that everything was fine, but Helena could tell Jureczek was in bad shape. She tried nursing him but he was slipping into unconsciousness. Helena was devastated. Just hours before, he had been crawling around, enjoying life, and now he was dying. At that time, Tadeusz was making his way to the hospital, but Jureczek died before he got there.

Helena insisted on remaining with Jureczek's little body but they wouldn't allow her to. Instead, they put Jureczek's body in the hospital morgue. It was December 4, 1947, St. Nicholas's Day, and their third son was gone.

They buried him in a little white casket at the Braintree cemetery. Helena put Jureczek's little gold baptismal cross around his neck. It was the only thing of value that was his while he was alive. She wanted him to have a possession of his own. A casket was not enough.

His death devastated everyone. Krystyna was especially affected and nearly had a nervous breakdown. She wouldn't speak to anyone. She would hide away from people, cry constantly, and was totally inconsolable. Although she was only three-and-a-half, she knew what death meant. She had loved her brother very deeply and now she knew he would never be with her again. Krystyna had been accustomed to holding and hugging little Jureczek, kissing his face while he patted her head. Now she was alone again and her loneliness overwhelmed her.

Tadeusz was in a state of shock. He had been studying English, but the death of his son caused him to forget everything. It was as though he were suffering from amnesia. Three of his children had died and none of it made any sense to him. His baby had been alive one day, and dead the next. He hadn't had enough time to prepare for his loss. Tadeusz had never told Helena of the old psychic's prophecy, but he finally did after Jureczek's death. He had been hoping that the old man, who had spoken to him so many years ago, was mistaken. Now he had to reevaluate his perceptions of life and reality and his perception of fate and prophecy.

The death of three of their children strengthened their beliefs in the importance of family. The love between parents and children, and all the precious moments they spent with each other, could never be replaced. It wasn't money, or a beautiful home that made a family happy. Happiness was all the moments when they laughed, sang, talked, and even cried together. That was what made them wealthy. Money was a replaceable commodity, people were not.

Soon after this tragedy, the small Szelazek family moved to the Polish Hostel in Kelvedon, near Colchester, in Essex County. The Kelvedon airfields still had aircraft carriers as well as Quonset huts on them. These huts were

Polish Hostel in Kelvedon, England—Quonset Hut Home for Krystyna, Helena, Jadwiga, Tadeusz, and pet ferret

being used as impromptu dwellings for the discharged Polish soldiers and their families. Helena and Tadeusz shared one of these huts with another family. The Quonset hut was not much of a shelter, but it was the Szelazek's new home. The building resembled a large metal oil drum, cut in half, lying on its side. It was definitely not a comfortable dwelling, especially in the winter; the freezing cold metal hut was no better than a refrigerator. The single thickness of its curved walls offered very little insulation from the winter cold. Often the water would be frozen in the basin when they awoke in the mornings. They had to cut wood for the stove, and sometimes, when they had a little money, they were able to supplement their heating fuel with coal. In the summer, the reverse held true: It was as hot as an oven inside the metal can. The small windows were insufficient to cool off the insufferable heat within.

Time passed and Helena became pregnant again. The baby was due in October and her grief was slightly lessened by the anticipated event. Helena had had a particularly difficult time dealing with Jureczek's death. She had always loved children and the loss of three sons was almost too much for her to bear. Now the new pregnancy gave her hope that the bad times were over for them.

Krystyna had been existing in a state of depression ever since the death of her brother. However, when she discovered that her mother was expecting, she began to show some enthusiasm for life again. Krystyna waited anxiously for the baby to be born and began to pick out names for her new sibling. All her favorite names were boys' names. Krystyna stated quite categorically that she did not want a sister. She would not choose a girl's name despite her parents' urgings. Finally, very grudgingly, she told her mother that she would allow her to have a girl. Helena had decided on the name Jadwiga (after a Polish monarch who had been a beloved ruler of Poland, and had been canonized a saint). Krystyna preferred the name Helena. She settled upon a middle name of Halina, when her mother told her that it would be too confusing to have two Helenas in the house. It was agreed upon, by all the parties involved, that the child would be called Jadwiga Halina. Her nickname would be Jadzia.

Early in October 1948, Helena went into labor. The pains were mild at first, so Tadeusz went to summon an ambulance. But the birth of their baby girl came quicker than the arrival of the vehicle. Helena was alone as Jadwiga was born, but she had no problem dealing with the whole event. She gave birth, cleaned off the baby, and then tied and cut the umbilical cord. All the previous knowledge and experience she had gained, by being a midwife to her aunt's children, was invaluable. She knew what to do for herself and she did it confidently. By the time Tadeusz and the medics arrived, Helena was able to hand her husband their new daughter. They were taken to the hospital in Braintree, Essex, where the doctors examined them both. Because the baby had been born on a Saturday, the hospital had not reserved any food rations for Helena's meals. She was able to nurse the baby even though she, herself, was hungry. As soon as the doctor declared them both healthy and fit, Helena insisted on leaving. She left the next morning, a little worse off for her stay, and more convinced than ever that it was best to keep away from hospitals.

~

Jobs in England were hard to come by after the war due to the influx of immigrants and for other economic reasons. Tadeusz began working at various odd jobs around the relocation camp and in the surrounding towns. He found work at a construction company that was laying sewer pipes and digging ditches. Occasionally he and Helena would go into the fields and pick produce with the other migrant workers. There were always vegetables to pick somewhere in the area. However, this meant that Tadeusz had to find some way for them to get to any of the available jobs. He solved his transportation problem by building a bicycle from old discarded parts that he found in the trash and at dumpsites. When it was completed, the bike worked so well that he began building more to sell to other workers who had no transportation.

Eventually, a little money began coming in as Tadeusz continued at the lucrative construction work and Helena found work on farms in the vicinity. The pay was decent, and sometimes the produce was free, which allowed Helena to supplement their diets with fresh vegetables. The children were thriving on this newly acquired bounty. Sometimes early in the morning, while everyone was still sleeping, Helena would slip out of the house and begin working in the fields. She would be back by 8:00 a.m., before the children awoke and Tadeusz left for work. It became a routine that brought in money, which they desperately needed; especially if they were to emigrate someday. Tadeusz felt that perhaps there were better economic prospects and opportunities elsewhere in the world. However, they were here for the present, and they made the best of the situation.

As Helena's field work became more consistent, sometimes Tadeusz joined her and worked on the large combines that harvested the wheat. He worked quickly and efficiently, which earned him a good day's wages, as well as bags of grain. With these, they could feed the few chickens they were raising at the hut. Sometimes he would help Helena pick vegetables, but his thoroughness would exasperate her. He refused to leave behind even a single pea on a bush, no matter how small. He acted as though the farm he was working belonged to him, and the farmer's loss of revenue from the overlooked peas was his direct responsibility. Needless to say, the couple's work ethic earned them a reputation among the English farmers. They were sought after to the exclusion of other migrant workers—Polish and English.

As time passed, things began to look up for the family. Tadeusz was hired as a full-time orderly at a nearby psychiatric hospital called Bridge Home, in Witham, Essex. He was soon entrusted with the care of some of the patients on the ward. Among these were some former soldiers who suffered from depression and war trauma. These Tadeusz treated with great empathy and consideration, often talking to them for hours to try to get them to cope with their lives. Tadeusz used all the insights he had gained about life, death, and fate to make sense of their shattered lives. The doctors would observe him with the inmates and soon realized that Tadeusz was obtaining wonderful results with some of their more difficult cases. Patients began to recover and leave the facility. Shortly thereafter, the staff began treating Tadeusz as a qualified psychiatric nurse. He was given a white uniform consisting of a well-tailored jacket, slacks, white gloves, and a shiny pair of shoes—much to the envy of some of the other orderlies.

There came a day when the chief of staff on Tadeusz's ward asked him to give his opinion on the old cases—patients who had been there for years. These were patients who seemed detached from reality; their behavior was often either borderline psychotic or almost comatose. The chief was interested in Tadeusz's opinion because he had noticed that the patients under Tadeusz's care behaved more normally than the patients on other wards. Tadeusz gave his opinions on each case and worked out a series of plans to achieve individual progress for the patients. Improvements in their conditions began almost immediately.

For instance, those patients who had been soiling themselves uncontrollably in the past were no longer having accidents. This seemed an almost miraculous turn of events to the chief of staff. Tadeusz explained that he had been rounding up all the patients on a regularly scheduled basis and ordering them to use the bathrooms whether they wanted to go or not. He had gotten them to relieve themselves immediately upon waking, soon after eating a meal, and so on. The enforced schedule was making the patients more aware of themselves and their bodily needs.

From Exile to Eden

They were developing a routine that worked for them. Tadeusz's no nonsense, "give 'em hell" language made the patients respect and sometimes fear him.

Tadeusz's method of bringing patients out of their lethargy was varied according to the patients. He found that some needed music, others needed gentle speech, and some needed confrontation to elicit results. The key was to become aware of the individual needs of each person and to respect them as people. The patients obeyed and respected him because of his fairness and consistency. Still not understanding how Tadeusz got the inmates to obey him, the British orderlies assumed it was through fear alone. They used to tell any unruly patients, "just wait till the Polak gets here, he'll hang you!" It wasn't the right way to handle the situation, but it always did the trick for them.

Among the population at the hospital were some perfectly normal people. Some were hiding from the stresses of life, while others had been put there by members of their family who found their presence inconvenient. There were titled or rich individuals who should have inherited estates, but instead were conveniently put away. There were wives who couldn't be divorced, but who were incarcerated by philandering husbands. There were ordinary people who were caught up in unfortunate disputes that cost them their freedom. They had basically given up, and felt they had nowhere to go, even if they were released. These patients had been living quietly among the psychiatric community, devoid of hope, until they met Tadeusz. His fierce determination and energy inspired them. Tadeusz played a key role in bringing their cases to the attention of doctors who then helped them gain their freedom and independence.

It was not in Tadeusz's nature to strike or abuse anyone, particularly patients. Even though other nurses did
so to maintain order, he only needed to talk and act
fiercely to get results. There was, however, one incident
on the ward that had Tadeusz act very much out of character. One particularly large, nasty-tempered patient on
the ward was making life miserable for all the inmates.
He should have been locked away in a criminally insane
ward, but for some reason, that was not the case. Tadeusz
was attempting to separate him from a group of inmates
whom he was harassing when the bully suddenly struck
out and punched Tadeusz in the face. Incensed, Tadeusz
chased the patient through two wards and finally caught
up with him in a corridor, where in spite of the man's size,
he was able to thrash the bully soundly. However, the
hospital's chief of staff observed the beating, and Tadeusz
was sure he was going to be fired when he was summoned to the chief's office. The doctor invited him to sit
down and then, after a little sociable small talk, he asked
Tadeusz why he had "disciplined" that patient so severely.
Tadeusz told him that throughout his life he had never
allowed anyone to dishonor him. No one, not even an
enemy during wartime, had ever had the nerve to strike
him in the face. He was not going to allow a bully to be
the first to have that privilege. The man needed to be
taught that he was responsible for his actions and all of
the subsequent consequences.

Expecting to be fired as a "subsequent consequence"
of his actions, he was shocked when the chief of staff
proposed sending Tadeusz to school to be trained as a
nurse. The chief would arrange for the hospital to pay for
his training. He had seen the potential in Tadeusz and
hoped he would go on to become a doctor of psychiatry.
However, Tadeusz had his sights set on emigrating from

Helena and Tadeusz in Kelvedon Settlement, Colchester, England

England. He saw no future in living on an island, even one as large as this one was. He informed the chief that his future was going to be elsewhere in the world, but he thanked him wholeheartedly for his generous offer and for his concern. The chief of staff wished him well and told him he'd do well in life no matter where his future took him.

Occasionally life would actually seem pleasant in the little English Quonset hut. The children would play in front of the house, feeding the pet ferret that Tadeusz used for rabbit hunting. They would laugh at its antics and fill the yard with happy noise. The surrounding countryside was quiet, green, and fruitful. Flowers disguised the drab living quarters, turning the improvised settlement into a little village. Life was not only back to normal, but also even joyful.

Helena became pregnant with her sixth child. She had been hoping for a son, but she knew this child would also be a girl. Helena went into labor at the end of January 1951. As was the case with most of her previous pregnancies, she never did make it into the hospital before the baby arrived. A baby girl, Elizabeth (Elzbieta), was born in the taxi cab on the way to the hospital in Colchester. Helena should have taken her straight home but decided to spend a couple of days in the hospital. The stay offered her a chance to pamper herself for a change. She had always been up and about immediately after giving birth and this rest was actually a novel change. English doctors always insisted that it was in the best interests of the mothers and newborn children to stay at least ten days in the hospital rather than get immediately back on their feet and back to work. Polish doctors, on the other hand, did not share this opinion. Polish women were ambulatory as soon as possible after giving birth, caring for their infants, and tending to the rest of the family. They were not treated with the same delicate consideration as the English women were used to. After two days, Helena insisted on leaving. It took very little persuasion for the resident Polish doctor to release Helena despite his English colleagues' opinions. Their stay had been brief, but long enough for the nurses to notice how bright and coordinated the newborn baby was. She was already following their movements with her eyes.

Helena and Tadeusz rejoiced over the new addition to the family. However, it was a brief joy. Within a few days, little Elizabeth began to act ill. She was cranky and out of sorts. The camp's doctor examined her and assumed it was pneumonia. He prescribed penicillin; then, when this didn't produce results, he increased the dosage. Still there was no effect. She had been taking the medication for long enough that the odor of penicillin was emanating from her little body, but the medicine didn't seem to be helping. Not only was she ill, but she was also developing new symptoms and side effects from the excessive amounts of antibiotics. She broke out in red spots, her skin and face were red, and she had developed a high temperature.

Dr. Pokorski readmitted Elizabeth to the hospital in Colchester. The situation became grave when it was revealed that all the infants who had been recently born or admitted to the hospital were dying of some kind of virus that was yet undetermined. The prognosis was poor since the doctors did not know what disease they were dealing with. They told Helena to be prepared for the death of her child. As a result, Tadeusz and Helena baptized her Elizabeth, in honor of the newly crowned Queen of England, in the hospital.

At this point, Helena was spending most of her time in the hospital. The staff had given their family the use of a waiting room. The children often took naps there while Helena spent time caring for Elizabeth, but things became worse when Krystyna and Jadwiga developed measles, which they contracted at the hospital. This was actually the second bout of measles for Krystyna, since she had had a mild case in Palestine. The doctors feared that Elizabeth might have also contracted measles along with the new virus.

It was then that Helena made an important decision. If Elizabeth was to die anyway, then she might as well die at home where she would be with her family. Helena would also be better able to care for the other sick members of the family. She took Elizabeth home and prepared for the worst.

As she worked around the house during the next few days, she kept the radio on quietly. It distracted her from her melancholy thoughts. The music was interrupted by a special medical bulletin originating from Madrid, Spain. It seems that a disease was discovered in the nurseries at various clinics, which was killing newborn infants. The symptoms were high fever, a red, flushed body, sleeplessness, and lack of appetite, among other symptoms. The illness sometimes resembled pneumonia, and at other times, it would attack the weakest organs or parts of the body. Penicillin was useless and Streptomycin was harmful. The doctors in Spain found that a new drug, Sulfanilamide, was effective in combating the disease. Helena was astounded. They had described Elizabeth's symptoms exactly. More astounding was the fact that she actually had the medicine in her suitcase. She had brought it with her from Palestine where she had gotten many different medications from the Hadassah. Helena had made it a habit to learn about as many diseases as possible and how to treat them. She kept various medicines on hand whenever possible. The habit paid off. She quickly dissolved the pills in some milk and forced it down the infant's throat. By the second dose, Elizabeth fell peacefully asleep. After a few days, her condition definitely improved.

It was several weeks later when Helena stopped in to see the children's pediatrician. She had come to obtain the medical records that they would need for the Customs Bureau. Dr. Pokorski saw her standing in the office.

"My sympathies. I heard your daughter had the virus that has killed so many children. When did she die?"

"She didn't die. My daughter is alive and healthy!"

"What? That's impossible! She had the same virus all the other babies had."

Apparently he had not received the bulletin, or had not had the time to read the newest medical reports. Helena filled him in on the report she had heard from Spain. He quickly took some notes and followed up with the staff at the hospital. She had given him some valuable information that day, which might have saved other children.

~

It seems that accidents and diseases were a constant reminder to the family that they were mortal. Sometime later, when Elizabeth was 11 months old, she became extremely curious and was beginning to walk on her own. She got into everything. Nothing in the little house remained untouched. Eventually, it was this curiosity that critically injured her.

Helena was boiling some milk on the stove when the toddler reached up and touched the handle of the pan. If Helena had not screamed out with fear at the sight, perhaps the child would have backed away. Instead, she tightened her grip on the handle and pulled it down.

The scalding milk spilled down her legs causing immediate damage. When Helena pulled the shoes and socks off her feet, the skin was already blistered. Helena immediately immersed her legs in cold water and the doctor was summoned to the hut. A doctor and nurse worked on the screaming child for what seemed like hours. They gave her medicine for the pain and ointment for the blistering. However, the doctor should have punctured the blisters and kept them dry and protected, but he did not. Shortly thereafter, the oozing skin began festering from the topical ointment. Elizabeth was still fortunate that, even though the burns were severe, she did not need skin grafts. However, some small scars remained as a reminder of the accident. It was a horrifying lesson to Helena who never again left pot handles so close to the edge of the stove.

≈ 25 ≈

Last Days in England

. . . opportunity presents itself.

Tadeusz and Helena often discussed the possibility of emigrating out of Great Britain. Some other Polish families in the settlement were already moving out to countries like Argentina, South Africa, Brazil, Australia, and the United States. The Szelazeks were undecided as to which country they preferred. Furthermore, not all of these countries appealed to Helena.

She had had a dream that she was herding cattle in Argentina and woke from the dream disgusted. She hadn't realized how much she despised shooing cows around. Later that day, Tadeusz mentioned that he had had a desire to move to Argentina and become a rancher. Helena's nightmare flashed vividly before her.

"If you want to move there, you can go alone. I have no intentions of herding more cows in my life. My entire youth was spent catering to those animals and I don't want to end my days looking at more of the same!"

There was no use trying to convince her otherwise and the matter was settled. Argentina was out of the picture.

Shortly thereafter, Helena heard from a neighbor that displaced Polish citizens could request immigration to any Allied or English speaking country. They would be issued visas and receive a small sum of money based on the distance (mileage from England to the country of choice). This would give them a start on a new life while they searched for employment. If they found a sponsor for their family—someone who would accept financial responsibility—it would be easier for them to procure a visa and passports. Some countries required sponsorship before they would accept any displaced person.

Helena requested immigration forms for Australia. She figured that, as the country furthest from England, she would get more money for their move. As to what they would do there when they arrived, she wasn't quite sure. She had always wanted to see a kangaroo. It was only by chance that a neighbor came by and gave Helena an interesting bit of news. Immigration papers to the United States were being halted within the next few days. So, if the family was interested in going to the U.S., they should get their papers in immediately.

Even though the news was not related to Australia, somehow this news seemed to prompt the family to reconsider their destination. They spoke to a priest by the name of Gogolinski who worked with the British embassy. He was helping Polish families immigrate to the U.S. The priest had a friend, John Maslanka, who was willing to sponsor the Szelazeks. If they were interested in settling in the U.S., they would move to Jackson, Michigan, where he lived. Although Tadeusz quickly turned in the required forms to the embassy, he soon discovered that the sponsor was pulling out of the arrangement. Maslanka was only interested in sponsoring Ukrainian families to the U.S. and would not sponsor any Poles.

Their moving plans seemed completely thwarted until Tadeusz remembered something important. There was still a chance that the move would go as planned. Tadeusz's parents and the Podlasek family had been friends and neighbors back in Poland. During the war, the Szelazek family helped the Podlaseks when they were short on food. They had undergone great financial losses at the hands of the Germans when their factory was confiscated. Then the Podlaseks were tossed off their land, which was given to a German family. Their money, their home, and their food eventually disappeared, so Franciszek Szelazek helped them in any way he could. Fortunately for the Szelazeks, the neighbor's son, George Podlasek, now owned a small business in a factory town called New Britain in Connecticut. Tadeusz contacted George, who agreed to be their sponsor. This meant he would have to give the U.S. government "assurance" that he was responsible for the family. George would be under contract to support the family if they were unable to support themselves. He would also be required to help them find jobs and to provide for any medical coverage. In this way, the U.S. government would not be responsible for the welfare of any immigrants. A huge wave of European immigrants, dislodged by war, was coming to American shores, and the economic strain was already being felt.

George Podlasek took a risk by sponsoring the family. It was a great responsibility and there weren't many honest people who would make such a commitment. Other sponsors merely signed papers but never followed through on their commitments, often forcing immigrants to fend for themselves in a strange country. But when George's mother heard that Tadeusz needed a favor, she urged her son to take financial responsibility for the Szelazek family as a special favor to herself. There was no way George could decline.

In order to immigrate to the United States, the Szelazek family had to get inoculations and complete medical examinations. These reports were then sent to the Emigration Commission in London. Unfortunately, when the deadline was almost upon them, Tadeusz became ill with the flu and could not make it into the doctor's office. Dr. Pokorski heard about their predicament and made a house call. He drew blood, gave inoculations, and filled out all the forms. Then he called up the Commission. The doctor informed them that he was sending in all the information, and would they please expedite all the paperwork as a personal favor to him. Dr. Pokorski was grateful to Helena for the information she had passed on to him and was doing his best to pay back the favor.

The move to the United States seemed destined to happen. Everything was falling into place within a very short period of time. People were helping them with the transportation costs, passports, and visas. Advice, assistance, and money were coming from all kinds of unexpected places. The doctors at the Bridge Home Psychiatric Hospital gave him a parting bonus of eight pounds sterling (a nice sum of money at the time). They were sorry to see him go and wished him well with his move to the "colonies."

So began the Szelazek family's journey to America, a place as close to heaven as they could let themselves imagine. A nightmarish journey had ripped them from their home in Poland, had taken them thousands of miles across the world, and had left them at this pivotal point in time. For years, their lives had been filled with death, hardship, and terror. Now, the New World would give future generations of Szelazeks opportunities no other place on earth could provide. This little group of pilgrims—Tadeusz, Helena, Krystyna, Jadwiga, and Elizabeth would be the first Szelazeks to live in the New World. It was a journey that was taking them from exile to Eden.

Part III

Coming to America:
Predictions Fulfilled

∾ 26 ∾

Life in the Tenements

. . . You will live and die in a foreign country.

A new chapter in the Szelazek family's life began with the long voyage to America. They departed England and crossed the Atlantic Ocean on the H.M.S. Mauritania during the month of January (1952). Their memories of that impressive vessel and the turbulent trip it made across the ocean would stay with them forever.

They were halfway through their journey to the port in New York when a violent winter storm hit, churning up the water like a washing machine. Hurricane-strength winds beat the waves into a frenzy of mountainous water, threatening to flip the ocean liner with every pounding blow. Many of the crew members on the Mauritania were young and inexperienced. By the time the tempest hit full force, they must have realized just how dangerous a sailor's life could be. They rushed to and fro, fear showing on some of their faces. As a result, it wasn't long before an atmosphere of panic began to spread among the passengers. The tension was heightened to new levels when huge waves began washing over the upper decks of the ocean liner.

The Szelazeks' small cabin seemed to provide them with a sense of security despite the storm, but Helena was worried and a little seasick. She was holding little Elizabeth, who was still recovering from the burns on her legs. The accident had occurred less than two months earlier, and she still suffered from pain and discomfort. The ship's doctor had provided Helena with some pain-killers, for which Helena had gladly given him $10 out of their scant funds. She had given Elizabeth some earlier; as they began to take affect, she tried to soothe Elizabeth with lullabies.

Jadzia and Krystyna stared out of the porthole at the water that sometimes covered the surface of the glass on the other side as little Elizabeth fussed and cried.

"Jadzia, get into the bed with your big sister." Helena said.

Helena's face looked worried and her voice sounded strained as she hummed church hymns. The cabin quieted down as the occupants listened to the sounds of the storm.

Tadeusz was not as easily persuaded to settle down for the approaching night. He was fascinated with the violence of the storm and studied it in a detached manner. While Helena watched the children, he left the confines of the small cabin and roamed the decks of the ship. The furious intensity of the storm showed his nature at the height of violence. Crashing waves periodically covered the ocean liner with walls of water. The winds howled, mingling with the noises of the ship. As he looked out the portholes of the lower decks, all that Tadeusz could see was gray, bubbling ocean water alternating with light from the dark gray sky. The vessel was bobbing like a cork in a bathtub.

Tadeusz attempted to remain on the upper decks where he could observe the storm. He even tried to make himself useful by trying to help out. It made more sense to him to be useful than to leave his welfare, and the welfare of his family, totally in the hands of others. Nevertheless, the crew insisted that all passengers stay in their rooms where they wouldn't be under foot. One of the sailors practically escorted Tadeusz back to his quarters. As they proceeded down below decks, he saw some emergency bailing equipment being assembled. Water occasionally washed inside the uppermost decks, spilling down stairwells. The situation was nerve-racking. Everyone on board had been ordered to put on lifejackets . . . just in case. Those who weren't vomiting from seasickness prayed or cried, though some were totally silent.

The Mauritania held together admirably, fighting its way through the rough waters of the Atlantic. Despite the passengers' visions of a reenactment of the Titanic, the fury of the storm abated. It had been a frightening experience, but it had ended without any casualties. The storm passed and the Szelazeks continued safely on toward their new home in America.

The Mauritania arrived in New York harbor on January 28, 1952. Tadeusz was 43 years old and Helena was 34. They were still a relatively young couple, but their tumultuous lives made them feel much older. They were starting a new life for their family in a strange, new country. The stress and responsibility that Tadeusz was feeling was tremendous: He had to protect a wife and three young children, he was unable to speak English, he was in unfamiliar surroundings, he had limited funds, and he had no job. The Szelazeks were beginning life in a land

R.M.S. Mauritania

that promised hope and permanency; they hoped their search for home was at an end.

The family gathered their possessions and soon passed through the Immigration Services office. They had a bit of trouble retrieving their baggage, however. This was

From Exile to Eden

because it was labeled with their original destination of Jackson, Michigan. As a result, Tadeusz had to tell the porters to offload the baggage, which had already been placed on the wrong train. Instead, they were moving to New Britain, Connecticut, where their new sponsor, George Podlasek lived. George's small factory, Winslow Automatics, was to provide Tadeusz with a job and an income. The whole undertaking sounded right and even a little poetic: They were in the process of moving from Great Britain to New Britain.

They put their bags in storage in New York and spent the night in a hotel because they needed to get in touch with George to let him know they were on their way so that he could make arrangements on his end.

The next day, they boarded a train and finished their journey. The train finally dropped the Szelazeks off at the Berlin station near New Britain, Connecticut. Andrew Podlasek, George's brother, met them there with his car. However, there wasn't enough room in it for the family and their suitcases. As a result, they had to store their baggage at the train station until Tadeusz could find someone with a station wagon to help him transport everything. Andrew then drove the family to the room George had arranged for them to stay in temporarily, which was in an already overcrowded apartment.

The room they rented was in a small, cold-water-only flat on North Street in New Britain. It was a cramped, cold room within a four-room apartment on the second floor of a two-story tenement building. The only heat source was an oil stove in the kitchen, and the only bathroom was a communal one that was in the hallway between the two apartments on the second floor. It was crowded, noisy, and uncomfortable. There was no privacy, and every aspect of their lives was exposed to people they would not have chosen to associate with in the best of circumstance—gossips, alcoholics, cruel and greedy abusers, and vulgar low-lifes.

One of the other rooms was occupied by a woman named Rybinska, another by a man named Wojdat, while a married couple, the Wyzykiewiczs, slept in the kitchen. The Wyzykiewiczs chose the kitchen because that meant they had a place to sleep for an insignificant rental fee. Their control of the kitchen also meant that they controlled the food in the refrigerator. Andrew Podlasek had dropped off $20 worth of groceries for the Szelazeks, which was a significant amount of food at the time; however, they never got to eat any of it. By the time Helena found out that the food was theirs, it had been eaten by the other tenants. That became an ongoing trend—the residents would often help themselves to the Szelazeks' food. They would all take advantage of Tadeusz's and Helena's generous natures with no reciprocation. Everyone acted as if it was absolutely natural to take what they wanted.

The Wyzykiewiczs were especially annoying in their behavior. One night was particularly memorable. It was extremely cold outside, so Mrs. Wyzykiewicz turned up the thermostat on the oil burning stove that stood in the middle of the kitchen. She forgot to turn it back down before she fell asleep. The stove started smoking, which soon filled the apartment with a cloud of black smoke. The fuel pump had jammed and the fuel oil was squirting out onto the floor. The stove itself was blazing hot and glowing red. For some reason, Krystyna woke up in the middle of the night and smelled the acrid smoke. She ran to wake up her parents who were already groggy from the smoke. Tadeusz immediately shut off the stove and Helena quickly bundled the children into a blanket and took them outside. A downstairs tenant, who acted as the superintendent, called the fire department. Although everything was under control by the time they arrived, all the tenants were told that it was fortunate that Krystyna woke up when she did. Everyone could have died that night.

When the superintendent (Mr. Latendro) accused the couple of carelessness, the Wyzykiewiczs blamed the Szelazeks for supposedly touching the stove even though it was they who were the ones sleeping in the kitchen.

"Those kids always get into mischief around here. They should be evicted. They're dirty. And they smear feces all over the walls."

At that, the landlord looked around the apartment. After noticing the blackened kitchen ceiling, he found the Szelazeks' room spotless. Helena had recently painted their room white (at her own expense), trying to make it appear larger and less cramped. The landlord saw all this, dismissed the accusations, repeated his warning to the Wyzykiewicz couple, and left. Now that their true feelings were out of the bag, the Wyzykiewiczs continued their spiteful behavior in a more open manner.

In addition to being crude and vulgar, the Wyzykiewiczs were also foul-mouthed in front of children. Mr. Wyzykiewicz would pretend to entertain them by telling them nursery rhymes. He would change the words to obscenities that the kids were unfamiliar with. Then he'd try to get them to repeat the rhymes. Tadeusz finally caught him in the act of this demeaning game and laid into him. He threatened to kill Mr. Wyzykiewicz if he ever dared to insult his family or dishonor their values again. Wyzykiewicz backed off after seeing the violence in Tadeusz's eyes. He knew Tadeusz meant it.

Eventually the Wyzykiewicz couple moved into the apartment across the hall with a Mrs. Micholek. This woman also proved to be of a twisted, cruel nature. She hated cats—and perhaps all animals in general—and she never passed up a chance to demonstrate her cruelty. She most definitely hated the stray cat that the three sisters had adopted. The cat lived outdoors in a small wooden crate where it would be protected from the elements, and it was the girls' closest friend in this new country.

One distressing day, the girls' pet cat became extremely ill and Helena watched as it vomited up its food. She could clearly see that the food contained pellets similar to rat poison. Fortunately, by emptying her stomach, the cat managed to get over the poisoning and regained her health. There was always the possibility that the cat had ingested the poison while scrounging for food, so no one was suspicious of foul play. A few months later, however, the cat became pregnant—much to the delight of the girls. It was then that Mrs. Micholek complained angrily to anyone that would listen.

"Someone should kill that cat. Now it's going to have kittens!"

When they were born, the girls kept watch over the newborn kittens. During this time, Helena allowed the new mother to stay in the attic of the old building. The girls saw her carefully carrying her kittens by the scruffs of their necks up the narrow staircase and were sure they would be safe there until they were old enough to feed themselves. However, a few weeks later, the mother cat became deathly ill. She had been fed poison once again, and the girls realized that she was dying. The baby kittens had nursed from her, and in turn, they had also been poisoned. They all died shortly after the mother cat died. Everyone in the Szelazek family cried—even stoic Tadeusz had tears in his eyes. There had been too much death over the years for the Szelazeks to ignore the loss of any kind of life.

Mrs. Micholek acted pleased when she heard that the cats were dead. To her, they were just useless animals that had been eliminated. For the Szelazek girls it was the death of a small bit of happiness that they had accidentally found in the friendless, inhospitable surroundings.

~

New Britain's claim to fame was that, at its peak, it was the Hardware Capital of the World—this meant it had more factories per square mile than anywhere else in the world. It spawned giants like Stanley Works, Fafnir Bearing, Atlantic Aerospace, United Technologies, and the list goes on.

The factories were mostly sweatshops that drained the life and energy out of the poor immigrants who worked within their walls. The overwhelming smells, heat, noise, glare, and congestion of these factories were oppressive. Employees suffered from many different maladies brought on by their employment. Yet, at the same time, working in factories was the only way that the poor, displaced Polish community could keep themselves fed and housed, and become integrated into the American dream. It was in this oppressive environment that Tadeusz, and eventually Helena, were driven to seek employment.

New Britain was a typical industrial city—overcrowded, dirty, and congested, and full of poverty, squalor, and disease. Its inner city bred both crime and illness. Tuberculosis was a constant scourge to the new immigrants who were crowded into small, confined communities. The Szelazeks were as careful as possible to avoid the company of people who were diagnosed with the disease. Most of the affected patients wound up in Norwich Hospital, where they would be treated for months on end. Poverty also created other illnesses in people—hopelessness, depression, alcoholism. The most frightening of the three was alcoholism.

After all the other tenants move out of the apartment, Tadeusz and Helena became saddled with the entire rental fee until they could locate new accommodations. During the interim, they sublet one of the bedrooms to an elderly American gentleman who helped offset some of the expenses. His actual age was difficult to estimate because he had abused his health to such a degree. He turned out to be an alcoholic whose family had abandoned him years earlier. He had a set routine of behavior that he would follow as soon as he collected his monthly disability check. He'd pay his rent fee first, and then he'd give a small amount for board. Helena would cook him meals, which he'd often skip because he was too drunk to eat. The old man would then spend the rest of his money on alcohol and his afternoons, evenings, and nights at the bar on their block. It was only a couple of buildings away, so he'd find his way home . . . usually.

Sometimes the Szelazeks would see him fast asleep on the stairs of their building, which was unfortunate because it was there that sometimes he'd be robbed by the other tenants. Tadeusz would take pity on him and drag him to his room. Because Tadeusz and Helena were so compassionate, they would also clean him up and feed him so that he wouldn't live on alcohol alone. Sometimes, the old man would try to give the Szelazeks his money when he was in one of his drunken stupors. They'd always stick it back into his pockets after he passed out. During the times when he lost all his money, he'd have to face withdrawal symptoms. The old man would get the DTs (delirium tremens), which were the most frightening to witness. He would cry, moan, scream, and see hallucinations. He would swear to anyone who would listen that he'd never drink again . . . empty words. Sometimes he'd manage to be sober for a few weeks, and then it would begin all over again. Eventually, the police picked him up and he wound up in a hospital somewhere. The experience of having an alcoholic living with them affected everyone. However, there was one positive outcome to such a negative experience. Helena and Tadeusz never had to convince their children to avoid alcohol.

⌒ 27 ⌒

A New Home

If you deal justly with others, treating them as you would want to be treated, you will be supported by God throughout your life.

American city life in the '50s was exciting, entertaining, and educational. By now the Szelazeks had been living in the United States for over a year, and they were becoming acquainted with everything that New Britain had to offer. They lived close enough to stores, schools, and everything they needed, so they always walked everywhere. If they needed to travel any great distance, taxi and bus transportation were cheap and convenient. The family loved the many city parks and took pleasant Sunday walks together; these walks created some of the happiest memories of the children's lives. Walnut Hill Park (with its monument, playgrounds, water fountains, rose gardens, trees, concert shell, and miles of green grass) was the family's favorite destination. In addition to the park, they enjoyed the library, the museums, movies, and Sunday picnics.

Not all the walks were pleasant, however. Helena spent hours walking from building to building, up and down every street, looking for an affordable place to rent for the family. No one seemed to want to rent to a family with three small children. Everywhere she went, the story was the same—no children, no pets. There were also some obvious cases of discrimination. Unfortunately many people felt that the "newcomers" were infringing upon the job opportunities and other rights of the American people. They were the DPs—the Displaced Persons—homeless and abused. People would even lie to Helena's face. They would tell her an apartment was for rent, start showing her around and then, when she told them she had children, they would say the place was already promised to someone else. At one house, a lady told her something she heard several times that day:

"Well, if you didn't have kids, we'd give you the apartment."

Helena finally couldn't take it any longer. She could not find a place to live because of the children she loved and fought so hard to keep alive.

"How did you manage to raise your children? Did you have a home to raise them in? You tell me you wish I didn't have any children. Well, if this is such a good thing, I wish the same to you. May your children die like mine died. Then you'll know how pleasant it is to live without them."

She walked out of the building, tears filling her eyes, as she headed for home. She hadn't walked far when she heard someone calling behind her.

"Lady! . . . Lady! . . . Stop for a minute! I know of a place where you can find rent."

The woman's guilty conscience prompted her to follow Helena. She told her about a rental on Clark Street where a vacancy had just opened up. Apparently she knew about an old man who had just died. His widow was moving out and was selling off all her furniture. The rental unit was in a dilapidated brick tenement building belonging to a man named Lipman who owned a large furniture store in downtown New Britain.

Everything worked out and the Szelazeks had a new home. The tenement building was only a block away from North Street, so the move was easily accomplished. Tadeusz bought all of the old lady's furniture for the exorbitant sum of $400. There was nothing of much value among the contents, but it got her out of the apartment all the quicker. Finally the Szelazeks had a bathroom within their own apartment!

Shortly after they moved to Clark Street, Tadeusz received a telegram that his father had died on December 24, 1953. Franciszek Szelazek had been 83 and had died from a blood clot that had been caused by a broken hipbone. Grandfather Franciszek had been hospitalized after the break for six weeks and everything had seemed to be healing nicely. It was Christmas Eve when he had finally been released from the hospital. He had been joking around with the nurses, happy to be going home, when the blood clot detached from the mended bone. It traveled to his brain and caused a massive stroke. He died on the steps of the hospital.

Everyone was shocked. Though the broken hip had been healing well, the clot had been an unforeseen tragedy. He had been in more serious accidents before and had lived through all of them—like the time his clothes had gotten caught in a threshing machine. In that accident, he had been mangled by the equipment and the horses. He would have died had it not been for the expert medical attention of his wife, Antonina, who was educated in homeopathic and herbal remedies. By applying her knowledge, she had stabilized his condition until it was possible to get him to a doctor. In comparison, this latest accident had seemed so minor. Antonina was devastated. Unwilling to live without him, she died of a broken heart on April 27, 1954, also at the age of 83.

Tadeusz grieved for his parents as best as he could. He wanted to be at his parents' funerals but did not have enough money to spare—certainly not enough to pay for airfare to Poland. His responsibilities to his wife and children prohibited him from dwelling upon his grievous loss too much. There were so many things he needed to deal with. The apartment they had moved into was a mess. The previous tenant had paid only $18 a month for the neglected rental. Yet, Lipman, the tenement building owner, raised the price to $50 without making any repairs or renovations. Tadeusz didn't complain; it was still cheaper than the dump they had moved out of. Nevertheless, the work it would take to clean up the place was daunting. The building was infested with rats and cockroaches. The woman upstairs never threw out her garbage, so the place was a breeding ground for all kinds of vermin.

Helena cleaned, painted, sprayed, exterminated, and did whatever she could to mask the smells coming from outside. She planted a window box around the wrought iron balcony on the front of their apartment building. Fresh cut flowers were always in a vase on the table, and the family dreamed of the day that they could have their own garden.

Lipman noticed the improvements to the apartment and raised the rent to $75 a month. He was the greediest man the Szelazeks had ever known. Although he was exceedingly wealthy—after all, he owned a furniture/appliance store and several buildings in town—he could extricate every last penny from a dying man . . . literally.

The Szelazeks found out that he had evicted the old lady from their apartment because the lease had been signed by her husband, not her. After her husband died, Lipman was able to break the lease and throw her out. He even swindled the Szelazeks out of money on a number of occasions. First, he sold them a stove for cooking and heating. Unfortunately it was set up for propane only, and all his apartments were set up for natural gas. He refused to take back the stove, or to have it altered for natural gas, so the Szelazeks were stuck with it. They were able to adjust it for heating and they could use the top burners to cook with, but baking was out of the question without calling in a repairman, which they could not afford to do.

The environment around the tenement house was dangerous and sometimes violent. People were raped, murdered, beaten, and robbed within these city blocks. After all, the Szelazeks lived in the heart of the city—in the heart of the slums. The local kids were, for the most part, a rough and brutal bunch. They'd throw rocks and punch each other in unprovoked rages. It reminded the Szelazeks of cornered rats in confined spaces. Often the girls were the targets, but on alternate days the neighborhood kids would be friendly and seek out the girls' company. It was a schizophrenic life, living among the slum kids.

The yard surrounding the brick tenement buildings had no grass or shrubs. It was a black asphalt area, crisscrossed with concrete sidewalks. There were two abandoned factories in the backyard, which were inhabited by homeless bums and sexual deviants. Women had been raped there. Helena rarely let her children out of her sight, but she couldn't be with them constantly. As a result, they had many traumatic, unpleasant, and frightening moments in their young lives. They could only dream of the day when they could afford to move into a better neighborhood and live the lives of all those people they saw on television.

However, not all the memories of Clark Street were unpleasant. There were some entertaining moments that the Szelazeks would always remember. At the very back of the property was a steep, asphalt-covered hill that the neighborhood kids used as a slide. They'd slide on anything that they could find—cardboard boxes, boards, and flat leather shoes. The asphalt would shred the boxes within an hour, but the experience was thrilling and demanding. If you fell, you'd be one large scab with bruises. A kid would be highly admired if he could negotiate the entire hill by sliding down it while standing up. The unabashed approval of the locals was well worth the ruination of your best shoes. Modern sports of skateboarding and snowboarding are easy when compared to facing the "rock mountain" of Clark Street.

Other entertainment included daydreaming in the burned-out car in the back lot. Within its blackened metal frame the girls would pretend to drive to distant foreign lands. They would envision lush forests, snow covered mountains, flower-covered fields, and never-ending oceans—they delighted in the pleasure of this imaginary world, as it gave them a chance to escape from reality. There were also high chain-link fences on which they could learn to be gymnasts. Sections of the fence were missing, so they could spin on the horizontal bars, and they could do flips, twirls, spins, and handstands. They could beat the other local kids in gymnastic routines that they made up spontaneously and executed regardless of danger to life and limb. It wasn't until years later that they saw the Olympics on television; there, to their surprise, all the gymnasts were re-creating moves that resembled their own crude efforts.

≈ 28 ≈

Brushes with Death

Your future is between you and God . . .

It was the summer of 1954. Krystyna was ten, Jadzia was nearly six, and Elizabeth was three. Helena went into the hospital for a fairly routine procedure to repair a minor hernia and some damage to her uterus. She had already given birth to six children and time had taken its toll. The procedure was simple and should have gone smoothly enough; but it didn't. Unfortunately, the anesthesiologist administered the spinal injection (epidural) incorrectly. Instead of being anesthetized, she was partially paralyzed. The paralysis twisted her hands and face as she lay there helplessly. They quickly checked Helena for polio hoping they could blame it on something other than incompetence, but they couldn't find anything else to blame it on other than the epidural. She wound up lying flat on her back for nearly a week while the paralysis slowly corrected itself. During this time, she was unable to see her children because it was against hospital policy.

When the ordeal was over, Dr. Bristol, her physician, told her that she should proceed with the originally scheduled operation. They should have left well enough alone, as it turned out.

The doctor allowed two of his resident interns to assist him during the operation. As the two students discussed the case, they felt fairly confident that Helena could not understand English; and they proceeded to crack obscene jokes about hysterectomies and female problems. Helena felt mortified.

To make matters worse, they botched this procedure as well. Helena knew something was wrong inside her as soon as she came out of the anesthesia. She was experiencing too much pain so soon after the operation. She kept telling the nursing staff that things just didn't feel right. They told her that they wouldn't give her any more painkillers. Neither the doctor, nor the nurses, believed that something was unusual or wrong. A couple of the nurses even called her hysterical and a hypochondriac. Then, as the pain increased, they turned off her call button so she wouldn't annoy them.

The result of this criminal neglect was that her stitches ruptured and the bed was covered in blood. Instead of informing the doctor, the nurses cleaned up the mess and told the doctor that everything was fine.

That evening Tadeusz came to visit her and was appalled at the change he saw in his wife. In a weak whisper she told him to listen carefully to what she was about to say.

"I am dying. No one wants to listen to me when I've asked for help. Take care of the children when I'm gone. Let them know how much I loved them. I love you Tadeusz, now and forever. Avenge my death!"

Tadeusz became frantic. Her lips were beginning to pale and her fingernails were turning blue. He sprang up shouting for help.

"I will not let them kill you. You will not die."

He grabbed the first person he saw outside of the doorway, who happened to be an Asian intern. Tadeusz pulled him into the room and shouted.

"My wife is dying. You will help her, now!"

The intern began to examine her and found that her blood pressure was critically low. He saw the disconnected call button and began shouting for the nurses. The first one that entered began to protest, objecting that he was not Helena's doctor. Another tried to tell him that Helena was just faking illness. The intern was appalled. He told them that he was going to report them; they were to call down to the operating room because the patient was dying. She was bleeding internally and she needed emergency surgery STAT.

He stayed with Tadeusz during the emergency procedure. He also kept going into the operating room to check with the doctors on Helena's condition and kept Tadeusz updated and comforted. He told Tadeusz that he would testify against all of the staff at New Britain General if Helena should die.

"I don't really care if they try to blackball me later. Here in the U.S., I am only an intern, but in China I was a doctor. I can always find some kind of work. I can't stand by and let them kill someone through neglect."

After the emergency operation, the hospital reluctantly contacted Dr. Bristol, who had done the original surgery. They had found a huge blood clot—the size of a goose egg—within Helena's pelvic cavity. Apparently a blood vessel had not been properly sutured. Helena could have died within a half hour if Tadeusz had not intervened on her behalf and if the intern had not been walking by her room at that exact moment.

Dr. Bristol apologized to Helena later the next day. He kissed her hand, and begged her forgiveness, saying that he was "not God." He then ordered her to be given a private room at the hospital's expense. After that, he demanded that the entire nursing staff on that floor apologize to Helena. Some of the nurses were upset and cried when they apologized, realizing too late that they could have caused her death. After that public apology, the nurses allowed her children to visit her whenever they wanted. (Eventually, the hospital changed its policy toward children visiting with their parents.)

Those horrible weeks of pain and fear became nightmares that stayed with Helena forever. Later in her life, whenever she received any shocks, or was frightened, stressed, or surprised, her spinal cord would spasm in pain. The site where the needle had been badly injected would continue to cause her discomfort throughout her life.

Helena came home from the hospital and slowly regained her strength. Tadeusz had changed his job and was no longer working at Winslow Automatics for George and Halina Podlasek. He knew that he'd neither get a promotion, nor anything more than minimum wage, if he had stayed. He had been required to do the dirtiest, most menial jobs in the factory—all the jobs no one else would touch. He knew that workers had flat out refused to do what he was required to do. The Podlaseks felt that Tadeusz owed them because they had sponsored his family's immigration to America. They had assumed that he would continue to work for them out of gratitude. Sponsoring the Szelazeks had not caused George any financial burden. And yet, in return for the kindness George had shown his family, Tadeusz continued to repay them many times over. Tadeusz was grateful to the

Podlaseks, but he was no longer willing to be taken advantage of. So, because his family's welfare came first, he took a job with Atlantic Machine and Tool Company (Budney's factory) in Newington, Connecticut. This company eventually became known as Atlantic Aerospace.

Tadeusz remained employed with this company until his retirement. In the meantime, the Szelazeks were trying to find better accommodations. Lipman, the landlord of their tenement building, had just informed them that he was going to raise the rent to $100 a month. The Szelazeks' budget could not withstand such a large increase in their rental expense. Helena knew she would have to endure another dreaded search, trying to find an apartment they could afford. It was merely a dream at this point to look at houses, which all seemed beyond their means. They had a small amount of cash in their savings account, which they had painfully accrued, but it was not enough for a down payment. Their hope was that perhaps someday they could afford some kind of fixer-upper house. Their hopes were always high; but so far, their luck had always been bad.

It was already the summer of 1956. One of Tadeusz's friends (Lewandowski) bought a new car, which he, unfortunately, never had a chance to drive. He was hospitalized with tuberculosis shortly after purchasing the car; so he asked his friend, Scierka, to drive it once in a while. It was not a very wise decision because Scierka liked to drink heavily. One warm Saturday afternoon, after Scierka had a couple of drinks, he stopped by the Szelazeks' apartment. On impulse, he asked Helena and Tadeusz to go for a ride for some ice cream at Guida's Dairy on Farmington Avenue. So, while Krystyna babysat for her younger sisters at home, they left with him in Lewandowski's new car.

Scierka chose a picturesque drive down Blake Road —a long road with many twists and turns. Unfortunately, even though he appeared to be sober, he was in no condition to drive a car. Scierka lost control at a sharp left turn at the bottom of a hill. The trees, which lined the road on either side, slowed the vehicle down as it plunged into the thicket. Some smaller trees snapped off as the car finally halted against a fairly large tree. The surrounding bushes sprang back up behind the tree, making the damaged car invisible from the road. Scierka and Tadeusz only sustained some bumps and scratches. However, Helena, who had been sitting in the front seat, received the full brunt of the impact. Her face had struck the dashboard, smashing out her teeth and breaking her jaw. Somehow she remained conscious, but Tadeusz knew that her injuries were serious. She had to get to the hospital fast. The road was lightly traveled; and since nobody could see them from the road, he decided to carry Helena out of the car and onto the street. Somehow Helena maintained consciousness and even managed to walk several yards down the road to an intersection.

A passing motorist stopped and rescued the blood-covered group. He drove them to New Britain General Hospital where the doctors began working on Helena's injuries. They set and wired her jaw and then began working on her broken ribs and internal injuries. In the meantime, Scierka downed several cups of coffee and was able to file an accident report. The Police accepted his concocted story and never found out that he had been drunk at the time of the accident. Tadeusz was too preoccupied with Helena's condition to be concerned with Scierka's problems.

After several weeks of sipping food through a straw, Helena was released from the hospital. She had to have all the remaining teeth in her mouth removed. Then she was fitted with both upper and lower sets of false teeth. The auto insurance paid for her bills and gave her a settlement of $7,000. This money, along with their other meager savings, totaled $8,000. This unplanned, but welcomed windfall was the exact amount that they needed to buy a house that had recently been put up for public auction. The family managed to occasionally find silver linings in all the black clouds that surrounded them.

⇐ 29 ⇒

Settling In

You will be . . . comfortable, happy.

A two-family house on Farmington Avenue in New Britain was being put up for auction after both owners had died. The couple had no next of kin to inherit the property, so the city put the house up for sale to recover back taxes. When Helena and Tadeusz discovered that the house was on the market, they put in a bid for $8,000. Miraculously, they acquired the property. The Szelazeks were finally able to move out of the slums of the city and into the suburbs of town. The house was an antiquated mess (built in 1909) but the price was right and the location was right.

In September of 1957, they moved into their "handyman special" home. The list of repairs seemed daunting, but the sight of trees, grass, and blue skies over their heads made the effort worthwhile. The old building needed new electrical wiring, new plumbing, a new septic system, a new roof, new windows, and a large amount of carpentry work. The house had once been a two-story single family dwelling that had been converted into a two-family house. The rooms were arranged in an awkward fashion as a result of the division, so walls had to be moved or ripped out. Helena worked on the walls: She removed lath and plaster, and nailed new plasterboard into place. Square corners were a challenge because none of the walls were flat or level. Somehow she managed to accomplish the impossible and made the walls appear smooth. A new coat of paint made everything appear perfect.

As for Tadeusz, he would work all day in the factory and then come home, eat a quick meal, and start working on wiring, plumbing, and carpentry. Everyone was expected to work including all three children. The kids were familiar with the tools and did their best to help out the adults. Working on the house was perfect on-the-job training for all of them and proved useful for many years to come.

The landscaping and yard work were the hardest parts of the repairs. The entire yard sloped steeply down toward the back, ending in a swampy mess that was lower than the surrounding area. The newer houses surrounding the Szelazeks turn-of-the-century home had their lawns and backyards built up much higher than the original lay of the land. To fix their backyard, the Szelazeks had to dump many tons of topsoil to level it out, nearly three feet above where it started. Helena and the kids raked the soil by hand, after the dump trucks deposited the costly mountains of dirt. They extracted all the rocks, which they saved to create the base for a driveway. It was backbreaking work for all of them; but since funds were limited, all the labor had to be done by the family.

After Helena mixed and poured cement into forms that Tadeusz built, she was able to reinforce the basement's crumbling stone foundation with a wall that was more than two feet thick. Covering the basement's dirt floor with concrete was next on the list of things to do. The family mixed and poured (by hand) a floor thick enough to divert the groundwater that flowed close beneath its surface. The floor they poured was a foot thick and had a drainage pipe that they could seal off with a screw-top cover, sealing the floor with a water-tight barrier when water levels rose after storms.

A stream crossed deep beneath the house and had always been an excellent source of water in the olden days . . . as the old well in the basement indicated. The subterranean flowing water kept the temperatures in the basement cool and uniform, which made it perfect for winemaking. Wine production began as soon as the grapes and fruit trees Tadeusz planted began bearing fruit. It was a family affair and the homemade wines they produced eventually became known throughout the state.

The list of tasks was never ending. After the house foundations were reinforced, they built a septic system and a leach field, and then they pushed the old barn back 15 feet from its original location to prepare for its conversion into a garage.

That last feat was an excellent example of the resourcefulness of the Szelazek family and their undaunted pursuit to accomplish the impossible. When they leveled the soil in the backyard, they had backfilled the barn with several feet of dirt above its original foundations. Tadeusz first reinforced the side walls, then he and Helena cut around the base of the structure. They used a beam and a section of tree trunk (a billet) to create a fulcrum; with this, the five members of the family were able to lift the entire structure up and onto a series of logs. Then, like the ancient Egyptians, they pushed the barn back to where they wanted it and set it into place. They then turned the barn into a garage with storage areas.

~

The Szelazek family had been granted citizenship on June 14, 1957, after months of grueling sessions that required memorizing facts about history and government. Krystyna and Jadwiga quizzed their parents on all the questions in the U.S. Citizenship booklet. They translated words, sentences, passages, and long paragraphs, hoping their parents could memorize as much of this difficult English language as possible. It was a frightening undertaking because Krystyna was only 13 and limited in her understanding of American civics. When the important day came, they were all nervous for their parents' success. If for any reason they didn't pass the test and they weren't accepted, the family would have to wait a few more years before they could try again for citizenship. Jadwiga kept asking her parents whether they would have to leave America if they failed the test.

During the testing, Helena and Tadeusz had to read a passage out of the U.S. Constitution and answer all the questions in the booklet. They needed to know about Congress, the Senate, the Bill of Rights, and all the myriad questions most average Americans cannot answer. They passed the test with flying colors!

Finally, all of the Szelazeks hard work and efforts had paid off. They became naturalized citizens and were no longer displaced persons. No one could call them DPs any longer. Even six-year-old Elizabeth signed her name on her citizenship certificate. It was the first official document of any sort that bore her signature. The Szelazeks finally belonged to a country and were happy to be home.

❧ 30 ❧

A Tragic Accident

We are all part of a scheme of existence . . .

Helena awoke one morning in May of 1958 and realized that she had had one of her prescient dreams
that warned her of imminent tragedy. It was the same
dream every time—she was picking blackberries. Whenever she found herself picking blackberries in her dreams,
someone in her family would be dead within three days.
It bothered her immensely that she could do nothing to
prevent the inevitable. She never knew which one of her
family members was in danger, and all she could do was
pray. The deaths of her father, mother, sister, and brother
were all preceded by the same dream.

In this particular dream, Helena dreamt that she was
about to pick the berries just as she normally did. Then,
the flow of the dream changed slightly—unlike in past
dreams, she hesitated, pulled her hand back and said,
"Not today." The hesitation puzzled her, and when she
awoke, she warned each of her immediate family members to be on their guard. She repeated the warning on
the following morning as well.

Three days after the dream, Helena was preparing to go to their bank, which was located a mile away. Ordinarily she could walk the distance in 15 or 20 minutes. The phone rang just before she closed the door and her heart immediately leapt to her throat. It was Krystyna, who, in a complete state of terror, was telling her that Elizabeth had been struck by a car that had run a red light. She thought that maybe Elizabeth was dead. Helena frantically began looking for her purse and house keys when there was another call from Krystyna. She told her that Elizabeth was not dead but that she had no eyes and no teeth. Not waiting to get any further updates on her daughter's condition, Helena ran the mile from her house to the corner of Grove and Broad Streets were the accident had occurred.

It had been the lunch hour at Sacred Heart School that her daughters attended. The three daughters had been waiting for the lunch hour to be over; and to occupy her time, Krystyna decided to mail a letter at the corner mailbox. Elizabeth tagged along behind her out of boredom. She was walking just a little behind Krystyna as they crossed the intersection at the stop light. Although the light was red for traffic and had a walk light, a drunken man in his speeding vehicle ran the light and struck Elizabeth.

The impact threw her across the street to the opposite corner. Her injuries were extensive. Elizabeth's heart stopped beating for nearly a minute. In addition, a broken rib punctured her right lung, two other ribs were broken, and some internal organs were injured; her front teeth were all broken, and some had been completely knocked out. Her face was covered with so much blood that the ambulance crew weren't sure what her features looked like or if she had been blinded.

When Helena came running up, a policeman had just loaded her battered child onto the stretcher and into the ambulance. She had run a mile in ten minutes, praying and crying the whole way.

Jadwiga was waiting for her sisters on the playground when she heard about the accident from some schoolmates. She ran to the scene just in time to see the ambulance leaving for the hospital with her mother and Elizabeth. Some people were telling her that Elizabeth was dead, others weren't sure. Finally, Jadwiga spotted Krystyna talking to a policeman; she was answering his questions and telling him details of the accident. Within a half an hour, Tadeusz arrived and left for New Britain General Hospital with Krystyna. Jadwiga was left behind and told to go back to school, as if that normal activity would help get her out of the state of shock that she was in. Instead, she was nearly paralyzed with fear, thinking about what it would be like to live without her sister. Jadwiga kept reciting a prayer over and over again. The candy taffy bar someone had handed her was clutched in her hand for hours until it melted, unnoticed by her.

In the New Britain General emergency room, a doctor told Helena that it would be an effort in futility to try and save her daughter's life. In his opinion, she was going to die. She was too critically injured and all that remained for Helena to do was to pray. Instead of listening to him, Helena began screaming that they had better get a specialist in immediately because Elizabeth was not going to die this day. Then Tadeusz arrived, demanding that they put her into an oxygen tent immediately while they were standing around waiting. It took a specialist surgeon 20 minutes to drive in from Hartford, by which time Elizabeth had become conscious again. She opened her blood-covered eyes and looked at her father. It was obvious that she wasn't blind.

The specialist, Dr Leonard Kemler, drained blood from her lungs and then worked on all her internal and external injuries. Dr. Kemler was an excellent surgeon with a generous, sympathetic nature. He told Tadeusz not to cry but to pray because she was in God's hands and not in his. She wound up on the critical list for nearly two weeks, but she did not die. Eventually, she made a satisfactory recovery. The doctor drove in from Hartford and visited her three more times to check on her progress. To everyone's surprise, he only charged $25 for his services.

As for the drunken driver, justice was never served. Despite the policeman's testimony that there were empty bottles strewn throughout the car, and that there was the smell of alcohol on his breath, he was not charged with drunken driving. He had a good lawyer and powerful friends in the local government, one of whom eventually became mayor of the city. They managed to keep the case out of court for nearly seven years through one legal maneuver or another. Incompetent lawyers, insensitive judges, and corrupt officials complicated what appeared to be a simple DUI case.

What complicated matters even more was the fact that neither Tadeusz nor Helena could speak English well enough to present their own case in court. They had to depend upon inexpensive and incompetent lawyers. Finally, in the end, they had to settle for a cash settlement of only $3,000. Their own lawyer told them to settle for that amount or they wouldn't get anything after the seven-year statute of limitations expired. The attorneys had dragged the case out for nearly that long, knowing the Szelazeks would have to settle for what they were offering. Needless to say, the money never covered all the medical expenses that the family had incurred. Instead it was held in trust for Elizabeth by the local circuit court judge, Henry Gwiazda, who did not even put this pitiful sum into an interest-accruing account. Elizabeth would have to wait until she was 21 before she could get the money.

☞ 31 ☜

Helena's Dreams

. . . that we cannot comprehend with our limited minds.

Tadeusz had his intuition, intelligence, and a strong
spiritual connection with his family to lead him
through the uncertainty of the future. Helena, however, possessed all those qualities and a few uncommon
ones as well. Her prescient dreams, psychically intuitive
moments, and strength of religious belief made her a rare
individual in her daughter's lives. The numerous strange,
inexplicable occurrences that constantly happened
around her made her daughters more open-minded than
most individuals. It also made them expect more detailed
answers and explanations from their religion, from science, their schools, the reference books they read, and
self-proclaimed gurus. Inevitably, all these sources fell
short of giving the girls any satisfactory answers. They
were always left with more questions than answers.

The resulting belief structure, which they created for
themselves, was based on their life experiences. It resembled a mixture of Eastern and Western religious philosophies. Their beliefs became a conglomerate of various
religions . . . whichever ones could best answer their

questions. They started with their family's strong belief in Polish Catholicism, with all of its Hebrew roots in mysticism, and to it they added Hindu beliefs in reincarnation, Chinese Taoist philosophies, and modern Spiritualism or New Age beliefs. They believed that since they were all the sum total of their life experiences, their philosophy was validated by their personally witnessed experiences. After all, one cannot deny the truth of that which is personally experienced and staring you in the face.

The family had witnessed Helena's blackberry warning dreams time and time again. After one such dream, Helena's sister, Stasia, died, and they watched their mother read the telegram, half relieved that it wasn't one of them who had died but someone in Poland. After another such dream, Helena's mother, Aniela, died on August 30, 1965, and then after yet another dream, her father, Wladyslaw, died on September 4th, 1979. All the children could do was comfort her because she could do nothing to change the future; nor could she warn anyone. She could only wait to find out who would die.

Usually Helena's dreams were everyday, regular dreams; they were filled with symbolism or were normal stress-related dreams. The normalcy of these dreams made most of them very difficult to interpret. In order for dreams to be interpreted, the dreamer has to be aware of all the nuances of their dreams that make them stand out as special. However, sometimes Helena's dreams were more specific in nature and content.

One occurred when Helena flew to Poland to visit her relatives in July of 1962. She dreamt that Jadwiga had been ironing in their upstairs attic bedroom when her iron exploded. By the time the Szelazeks received her letter containing this dream, something very similar had already occurred. Jadwiga had indeed been ironing when the iron began acting funny—sporadically going on and off. She picked up the extension cord and was checking the connection when the outlet cord exploded in her hand. The small explosion, complete with sparks, sent out bits of flying plastic and metal that cut into her finger. That experience, plus a mild electric shock, discouraged her from plugging in any appliances for at least a year. Fortunately for Jadwiga, it was a phobia that was short lived.

Helena also had a couple of experiences that could have been NDEs (Near Death Experiences). The phrase Near Death Experience was coined by Raymond Moody, PhD., who has written several books upon the subject. (Jadwiga had an opportunity to speak with him in November of 1992. He verified her family's conclusions upon the matter of NDEs.) After both of her NDEs, Helena would return (awaken) all stiff and in pain. The memories that she retained from the experiences were usually very profound and contained stunning information and vivid descriptions of what she saw.

One such experience occurred in 1978, when her family believes that she had her first serious heart attack in her sleep. Helena had not been feeling well when she went to bed that night. She had many stressful situations that she encountered on a daily basis, and because she was such an empathetic person, life began taking a toll on her and on her heart. That evening, she fell asleep and immediately felt that this sleep was different than usual. She was totally aware and felt herself walking through a misty, foggy area. Groups of people were waiting on the outskirts, huddled together, or were walking toward the center of a gathering in a bright area further on. A dark-haired man extricated himself from the crowd and bounded joyfully toward her.

"I finally found you! I've waited and looked for you for years! What? Don't you recognize me? I'm your husband and you're my wife. Don't you remember that we drowned on the ship together?"

With a shock, Helena realized that this truly was the man she had been married to in her previous lifetime. He clutched her by the arm and delightfully declared that now they could be together at last. In that precise moment, she realized that she had died. Helena's response was immediate.

"No! I have a husband now and children. It is the children who I cannot leave. They need me!"

She felt his unhappiness at her words. Helena would have liked to have supported his joyful reunion with her; but her acceptance of the afterlife was impossible under the circumstances. She just couldn't be dead right now. She then saw a figure standing tall above the crowd as though upon a brightly lit hill. There was a circle of shining beings and people around him—men, women, and children. She realized that this was Jesus in normal attire. He looked like a normal human being but was glowing with light. When she saw him, Helena broke away from her "husband" and ran directly to the figure; she then fell on her knees, and began pleading:

"He seems so happy to see me and he wants me to stay with him, but I have a family, and I want to stay with my children. They still need me and I love them too much to leave."

Jesus smiled and reassured her.

"Don't worry. You don't have to stay here with us right now. You can choose to go back. You will know when the time is right for you to return."

Helena thanked Him and began running back in the direction from which she had come. She felt herself falling and then she landed with a thud back into her body on the bed. She was totally stiff. She couldn't move an arm or a leg and she couldn't make a sound. Slowly she began moving one finger; she worked at it until she could move her hand, and then she moved her arm. She grabbed Tadeusz's arm as he lay next to her. She tried to speak but was unable, so she had to wait until he became aware what was going on. He quickly realized that she was practically paralyzed, and he began massaging her limbs and moving her around the room until it passed. It is likely that Helena had had a heart attack and had lived through it. She had been allowed to return to those she loved.

Helena realized a few things from that unique experience. She had seen Jesus because he represented all that stood for the highest good in her life. Perhaps some souls would have been met by Mohammad, others by saints, holy men, or Jehovah himself. Even those who did not believe in any organized religion would have been met by someone they loved—someone who would lead them through the new experience of death, or life after death.

She also realized that we all love each other unequally. Why hadn't she loved her previous husband enough to stay behind with him? And did she now love her present husband less because she briefly felt something more for the previous one? How very confusing. . . . Yet, she decided, if we can be accused of not loving equally, and hurting others in the process, we must also be more forgiving and understanding when we ourselves are slighted, hurt, and unloved by those we hold most dear. She realized that this was a difficult lesson to absorb for many and she knew that there is so much we do not understand.

32

The Expanding Family

Wealth means different things to different people.

In April of 1975, after 25 years, Tadeusz Szelazek finally retired from his job at Atlantic Machine and Tool Company. It had been a tedious, difficult, and dirty means of employment, but it had provided money to put food on the table, provide an education for his children, and ensure excellent possibilities for their future. He had been a precision tool grinder for all of those years and was grateful that he had been able to provide for his family. His inability to speak perfect English had prohibited him from working at jobs more suited to his intellect. However, he always rationalized away the bitterness by appreciating the good income derived from menial labor and the satisfaction of doing a job well. He was not wealthy in the traditional sense of the word, but he was well off enough, comfortable, and happy. He had achieved it all through hard work and honorable choices without walking on other people's backs.

As the daughters' finances stabilized in addition to their parents', the Szelazeks were even more driven to make their family prosper. The daughters saved all their individual paychecks and contributed them into a joint family fund. Even the money they earned from their after-school jobs and private tutoring work went into the communal kitty. It was extraordinary, by normal standards of the day, that each was able to begin married life with mortgage-free homes while they were still in their early 20s.

In 1969, the Szelazek family bought a second house on Shenfield Street when Elizabeth married Gerard (Jerry) Emerson. They had an only son, Adam Charles Emerson. Elizabeth had graduated with honors (cum laude) from Central Connecticut State University (CCSU) with a Bachelor of Science degree in the Fine Arts. She went on to get her Masters degree and taught in the New Britain School District, where she still teaches today.

Then, in 1973, the Szelazek family bought a third home on Garden Street for Krystyna and her family. Krystyna graduated from the University of Hartford and went on to get her Masters degree in English. She married Leonard Fiedorczyk in 1971 and had two children, Henry Fiedorczyk and Ann Marie Fiedorczyk.

Jadwiga married Douglas Morrison in 1971 and then lived in Hawaii for two years, while he served in the U.S. Coast Guard. Eventually, sometime after they returned, the house on Farmington Avenue was given to the two of them. They had two children, Douglas Alexander Tadeusz Morrison and Elisa Jadwiga Morrison. Jadwiga received her Liberal Arts degree in English and History from CCSU and went on to work in business and school administration. It was during her return to Hawaii in 2000 that she had time to write this biographical journal of her parents' lives.

As for the lives of the three Szelazek siblings, they have many interesting tales of their own; apart from their parents' experiences. Perhaps those experiences will be told in their own memoirs; but this book is primarily Helena and Tadeusz's story, as the predictions of Symbolerus unfolded.

⌐ 33 ⌐

Where There Is a Will
There Is a Way

You will die at the age of 72.

It seemed that only one of Symbolerus' predictions was yet to be fulfilled. All the others had come to fruition. The Szelazeks often wondered whether Tadeusz's life would end at 72, or whether there would be extenuating circumstances that would prolong his life. Still, it was not a question they dwelt upon.

Tadeusz's health had become less robust after his retirement. Arthritis had twisted both his hands and had settled into his left hip, but he kept on working around the house and the garden. Retirement allowed him to indulge in his hobbies . . . like winemaking. His home-made wines became legendary in the town of New Britain. The whole family was involved in the process: you could see him trimming the grape vines, or perched on a ladder, hanging out of a cherry tree; Helena would clean and press the fruit and process the juice for wine; and, the girls, despite their newly acquired status as wives and mothers, continued the seemingly never-ending process of picking fruit for the wines.

Tadeusz's third grandson, Douglas, provided him with the opportunity to lavish his attention upon another generation of Szelazeks because at this time Jadwiga and her husband lived on the first floor of the Farmington Avenue home, while Helena and Tadeusz still lived on the second. This proximity allowed Tadeusz to take the toddler on long walks in his stroller. Then they would sit together under the grape arbor, as he told Dougie stories about things that he could not yet comprehend. He developed a strong bond with this grandchild . . . a bond that played an important role in their futures.

One sunny October day in 1982 when Douglas was 17 months old and Tadeusz had just finished his 72nd year of life, they were both sitting under the grape arbor near the house. Dougie suddenly became very still in his seat and began following something with his eyes. As the child's eyes traveled in the direction of Tadeusz, Tadeusz suddenly felt a presence near him. Dougie's face broke into a smile as he also acknowledged someone else's presence. Later that evening, Tadeusz remarked to Helena that he had had the eerie feeling that his deceased mother had visited them. His mother had often appeared during times of imminent danger, or serious circumstances, to warn him and to keep him safe. Even though Tadeusz was a little disconcerted, he felt even more surprised that little Dougie appeared to have seen the spirit.

The next morning, Helena came banging on Jadwiga's door.

"Jadzia, come quickly. There is something wrong with your dad. He is acting confused . . . he remembers things from the past, but no recent events. He does not remember that we built an addition onto the house two years ago. He had to touch the walls with his hand to convince his eyes. He keeps repeating that there is some-thing wrong with him."

Jadwiga knew right away that he was having a stroke, or something similar. She drove him to the hospital emer-gency room as quickly as possible. During the entire trip, she tried to reassure him and keep him focused on the present. She knew that if she could get him to understand his importance to their family and to the grandchild he idolized, that she could keep him attached to this life just a little longer. Jadwiga told him that he had unfinished business in this world and that Dougie still needed him. She made him promise her that he would not die; and she kept him repeating that promise over and over again. When they reached New Britain General Hospital, she had hoped that the emergency room staff would jump on the crisis immediately. Instead, because he had walked in under his own power and he wasn't visibly bleeding or in pain, they ignored him for nearly an hour. By that time, by shear willpower, he began returning to normal. The examining doctor finally arrived and said that his con-dition looked serious. Tadeusz showed all indications of heart problems, a possible minor stroke, a possible blood clot or aneurysm, or some other type of serious situation. The doctor said that he was going to check him into the hospital immediately for testing. Tadeusz gave him a con-descending look.

"I don't need you, or your services, any longer. You should have helped me an hour ago. I'm not in danger any longer. I gave my daughter a promise that I will live and I am going to do just that."

With that, he got off the examining table and walked out of the hospital. It was no wonder that he didn't have room in his life for doctors. They had seldom been of any help to him.

After Jadwiga got him settled into the car, he said that he remembered giving her his word that he was going to live; and that she had something important to tell him. He wanted to know what it was that was going to keep him attached to the living for a little while longer. She then told him what his promise was for.

"You cannot leave us until you teach everything you know to Dougie. And, while you're at it, you'll have to be here for my other child as well, because I am pregnant. You now have too many unfinished commitments in life and you need to help me write a book about our family's saga. I now have your promise, which you solemnly swore to, and you can't fail me. You can't leave us."

With that he kissed her hand, smiled with tear-filled eyes, and lived for another ten years—despite a body that should not have allowed him to live. The last three years ended up being a medical miracle because one of the valves in his heart wasn't even working properly.

≈ 34 ≈

Tying Up Loose Ends

If you find that, at the appointed time, there is something that you have to accomplish, something that will be of service to God and man, your time will be extended.

By 1983, Jadwiga's small family of four moved out of New Britain into a house they had built in the town of Avon, Connecticut. She was still able to visit her parents daily at the old homestead, however. During this time, there were many family gatherings and many impromptu discussions regarding metaphysics and spiritualism. On one particular afternoon, Elizabeth and Jadwiga were discussing what the basis of power was for the execution of table-tapping. Was it physical power using the body's electricity, or was it produced by harnessing outside forces? They were determined to have their mother, Helena, demonstrate her ability. It had been decades since she had allowed herself to use her skills, mainly because she still was worried that she might be putting unseen souls at risk. Perhaps by communicating with the deceased purely for entertainment or curiosity, she might be needlessly putting them in harms' way, and she wouldn't do that for any reason. However, her two daughters were persistent and they won out in the end.

The three of them sat at the heavy, old, oak kitchen table. Jadwiga sat on the right, Helena in the middle, and Elizabeth on the end. Helena put her fingertips on the edge of the table and began concentrating. After a little while, the table began to creak with little movement noises.

"This is definitely not like it was before. I must be getting too old because it hasn't lifted up yet."

In her daughters' minds, however, just the creaking was an exciting display. Suddenly, the entire table slid back toward them, at an angle, pushing Elizabeth back by at least a foot. It was as though someone had slightly lifted and then pushed the table into her. All Helena said was that it was not a very good display. Then her head began to ache and her daughters told her not to exert herself further. They realized that they had finally seen, first-hand, a display of what they had always taken for granted, but never witnessed . . . until that day.

They knew that their father also possessed unusual skills. However, these were more skills of intellect rather than psychic powers. Tadeusz could analyze a given situation and get down to the bottom of any complex issue with the simplest of words. His discourses on life, philosophy, religion, science, and other subjects always provoked a lively discussion. His company was eagerly sought out by many people—whether they agreed or disagreed with him. The pursuit of knowledge, especially when you are surrounded by those who love intelligent conversations, is a pleasure beyond measure. Even as children, the Szelazek girls would quietly eavesdrop on such conversations from their rooms, tallying up the rebuttal points like a sports game.

One of Tadeusz's favorite debating partners was a gentleman who rented the upstairs apartment in their old home on Farmington Avenue. Mr. Smialkowski was well versed in theology because he had once contemplated a career in the priesthood. His personal disillusionment over the years left him a skeptic and doubtful of concepts such as the existence of God or the immortality of the spirit—that is, life after death. Their arguments and discussions often became heated, but were fascinating. They would usually end with Smialkowski uttering the same statement:

"When you die, you can come back and let me know it's for real."

"I'll do that," Tadeusz would answer.

His unwavering belief was based on a lifetime of experiences. After all, our opinions and beliefs are a direct result of what we have lived through. Tadeusz's life experience was more unusual than the average person's and that led to his unique perception of what the universe was all about, what he believed that God really was, and what he thought the meaning of life was.

To Tadeusz, God was expressed as the Light, the spark of creation, containing all within itself—logic, wisdom, power, creation, destruction, mutation, the positive, the negative, the yin and the yang. All living things contained souls, or that spark of energy, which was a part of God. To him God was not your typical white-bearded, personal God replete with human qualities and human shortcomings. Instead, He was the energy that created this world, the singularity that is the beginning point of creation in the universe, that which is within all things and that is the sum total of all atoms that connects all animate and inanimate matter. It is within this "soup" of energy that His power can be felt, His connection to us can be understood, and His strength can be called upon and harnessed through prayer in times of need. It was this belief in God that protected him and brought him through his times of grief. It was a belief he never lost in this lifetime.

It was prayer that kept Helena and Tadeusz alive despite all odds. Hope, security, and trust in God were expressed in their prayers. In recent scientific studies, it has finally been established that prayer can affect more than the strength of our faith or the state of our souls. The concept of prayer, as being a valuable tool in the healing of our bodies, is now being incorporated into a discipline of study called psychoneuroimmunology (PNI) by the scientific community. According to the Mosby Medical dictionary (eighth edition, 2009), psychoneuro-immunology is a discipline that studies the relationships between psychological states and immune responses. Author and NPR religion correspondent, Barbara Bradley Hagerty, expounds upon this discipline stating that she feels that prayer can affect the immune system, creating either health or disease in the body. She says in Chapter 3 of her book, *Fingerprints of God: The Search for the Science of Spirituality*, that "What was once superstition is now accepted science: our thoughts affect us on a cellular level, unfolding the biology of belief."[8] Positive thinking results in health, negative thinking result in ill health. Prayer is positive thinking and can help people cope with their lives and health issues.

---

8 Hagerty, B. (*Fingerprints of God: The Search for the Science of Spirituality*, New York 2009)

Prayer and positive thinking were what helped Tadeusz in his final years on this earth. By 1989, Tadeusz's health was failing considerably. Dr. Slysz, his physician, tried to persuade him to get an operation on the faulty valve in his heart. However, Tadeusz refused any invasive operations, knowing that he had already extended his life beyond its normal span, as a direct blessing from God. Instead, Dr. Slysz prescribed him an oral placebo-like medicine. He commented:

"He is not alive because of the pills I've been giving him. He is a walking miracle and I don't know why he's still alive. If I knew what was keeping him alive, I'd prescribe it to others."

Nevertheless, Tadeusz lived because he needed to put his affairs in order and he felt he still had some obligations that he could not leave undone. In his final years, he began tidying up loose ends of unfinished personal and financial business, which would benefit the family after he died. He knew he was entitled to a retirement pension from England, which he had not yet taken advantage of but decided to apply for. He knew that income would come in handy as additional retirement funds for Helena. Also, his family wanted to make a display case of all the medals he had been awarded during WWII. Over the years, his medals had been lost during travel, frequent moves, and the children's playful curiosity. They discovered they could all be replaced by sending requests to the British government, which had his records and medals on file. The family succeeded in obtaining all the medals in the spring of 1992.

After Jadwiga's short-lived move to Chicago (1987–89), she and her family moved back to Burlington, Connecticut. For three years, she would visit with her father, open his mail, fill out insurance forms, discuss medicines, recopy notes from his memoirs, and try to make his last days pleasant. She provided him with oxygen to make his breathing easier and a walker with which he could support himself.

In July of 1992 the family planned a party to celebrate his 83rd birthday, which he knew would be his last. They invited everyone he knew and he was looking forward to saying his final farewells in person.

The day of the party was beautiful. Tadeusz felt better than he had in years. He got dressed in his best suit and tie, exchanged the walker for a cane, and felt good enough to forego the oxygen. The party was held at Jadwiga's house in Burlington, where Tadeusz greeted every invited guest at the door. He joked with everyone and laughed at the candles his family placed on his cake—38 with his age in reverse. Then, at the end of the day, he was the last to leave, making sure that he bade every one of his guests a final farewell. He had told his guests that this would be his last birthday celebration. Everyone tried to assure him that he was wrong. His tenant, Smialkowski, commented that if this was Tadeusz's last birthday, then they would all soon know what was awaiting all of them—if there truly was life after death. He said that if anyone could tell them, then it would be Tadeusz. They all joked about Houdini and secret passwords they'd use to verify identities after death.

By the next day, there was blood in Tadeusz's urine as his kidneys began shutting down. Within three days, he was back on oxygen and beginning to experience pain and shortness of breath. Later that week, Jadwiga was talking with him about the benefits of hypnosis and meditation and how she could help him relieve some of his pain with guided meditation. (Jadwiga was a certified hypnotherapist by this time.) He had been unable to sleep because of his discomfort, so he agreed to try whatever solution she could manage to come up with to help him rest. The session worked well and he was dozing peacefully when Jadwiga went out to pick up the mail for that day. Among the envelopes was a notice stating that both Tadeusz and Helena qualified for British social security, and that they would begin receiving a check within the month. It also clarified that Helena would receive her husband's portion upon his death.

When he awoke, Jadwiga told him the good news. He sighed, thanked God, and said that everything in his life was now in order. He felt that everyone he loved was finally in a good place, and that his family could now take care of themselves without him. The only thing he regretted was that his youngest daughter, Elizabeth, was unhappy. She and Jerry had divorced a few years earlier, and things were presently very difficult for her. Tadeusz was at a loss as to how to help her. Jadwiga assured him that everyone was fine and that he should rest.

He was dozing when suddenly his body began convulsing. His eyes rolled back in his head and his breathing became ragged. At this point, it became obvious that the oxygen was not helping and Jadwiga immediately called an ambulance. At the hospital, the staff eased his pain with drugs and his family was able to converse with him until they gave him morphine for the ever-increasing pain. Whenever he came out of the morphine-induced sleep, he'd express his concern for his family and his gratitude for having them all around him. His cardiologist, Dr. Charles Leach, gave him a private room where his family could stay with him and where Helena could rest on the adjoining bed. He instructed the nurses to comply with whatever his family requested. It was the gracious kindness and sympathy that Dr. Leach showed the Szelazeks, both young and old, for which they will always be grateful.

Tadeusz's last moments were a monument to the strength of his convictions and beliefs. At one point, his heart stopped beating, and then when it began again, we saw him smile as he murmured "Mama." He must have been in the presence of his mother whom he had loved beyond all measure. Again his heart stopped. A half a minute later, it restarted. He opened his eyes, threw his arm around Helena with a strength that came from beyond him (he actually bent the needle in his arm). He held her to him and told her that he loved her. He finally died at 10:00 p.m. on August 4, 1992.

When the family finally returned home, it was already around midnight. Smialkowski was waiting for them as they got out of the car. He was agitated and trembling. He wanted to know precisely what time Tadeusz had died and asked if it had occurred at 10:00 p.m. When they said yes, he took them upstairs to his apartment and showed them a shattered light bulb hanging from the fixture on the bathroom ceiling.

"At 10:00 I was in the bathroom when the light over my head exploded. I knew immediately that my friend had died. He gave me a sign as I had asked him for."

Jadwiga did not go to sleep that night. Instead, she sat in her living room, and cried for the loss of her dearest father. She had the television on quietly in the background to keep her company as she lay resting on the couch. Then, for no reason at all, the television began scrolling from one channel to the next all by itself. She smiled through her tears and told her father that it was not necessary to prove anything to her. She knew he was okay and that she would always love him until the day they met again. At that, the television stopped its scrolling and remained on one station.

It has often been theorized that the easiest way for a spirit to communicate, shortly after death, is through some electrical means. After all, we are all just energy beings, so it stands to reason that manipulating electrical devices would be the first and easiest means of communication. Time after time, Jadwiga has seen just this sort of anomaly when she has been confronted with the deaths of her dearest family and friends. She believes the soul lives on when the body no longer functions.

☞ 35 ☜

Fulfilling the Prophecy

He can be found everywhere.

Tadeusz Szelazek's funeral was a splendid affair. The flowers filled the room, and the largest, most beautiful bouquet was a display that came from Smialkowski. It had a card addressed to his good friend, Tadeusz. On it he thanked his true friend for giving him the gift of an answer to his questions.

Businessmen, dignitaries, and politicians from the entire state gathered at the service—the mayor, former mayors, the current congressman and senator. It was a special gathering honoring Tadeusz by everyone who knew him. The line of cars that began at the funeral home stretched for blocks through the city, as it traveled from the church to the cemetery. At the cemetery, a military honor guard gave him a 21-gun salute, and the eulogy was given by his good friend, Judge Henry Gwiazda.

"My good friend is dead. We had an agreement that whoever remained behind would speak at the other's funeral. I am sad to say that it is my honor to do so. Tadeusz came to this country as a 'displaced person' or a DP. I always believed that stood for Delayed Pilgrim.

259

The newspapers made an error in the obituary and said that Tadeusz was *exported* to Siberia in 1940. I believe that every place on earth, including Siberia, needed a man like Tadeusz to live in their country. He was truly an export worthy of possessing . . . . Now, God has him in heaven."

The judge then went on; he talked about his friend, giving him the homage he deserved in life and in death.

Many photos were taken at the church and the gravesite. Some of those pictures were sent to distant friends and relatives. Among those friends were the Podlaseks and their relatives the Kacickis, who now lived in Arizona. (Grazyna Kaciciki was Halina Podlasek's daughter, and Grazyna's son was Zygmunt Kacicki). When Halina Podlasek received the photos from the funeral, she happened to show them to her visiting grandson, Zygmunt Kacicki. This was the same Zygmunt who had been engaged to Elizabeth before she had married Jerry Emerson. The engagement had been terminated under some unhappy circumstances and some misunderstandings while Zygmunt was serving in the Air Force during the Vietnam War. Now, as he stood looking at the photos of the funeral, he saw Elizabeth again after 25 years. He added a postscript to the condolence card his family sent back to Connecticut. He gave Elizabeth his telephone number and his address in Florida.

Elizabeth had never expected the surprise that awaited her when her family received this card. She had lost track of her old beau and never thought she would hear from him again. She ended up calling Zyg in Florida, and within minutes, they made plans to visit each other. When he arrived in Connecticut, a month later, he proclaimed that he had always loved her, and despite his previous marriages, he had never stopped thinking of her. In fact, he said, he had tried to find her within each of his relationships, but never could do so . . . which is why his relationships never worked out for him. He then produced her old engagement ring and asked her to marry him again. They were married within three months, on Valentine's Day, 1993. He then told her, with great hesitancy, about a lucid dream he had had before the funeral photos reached Arizona.

Zygmunt had dreamt that Tadeusz walked into his kitchen, put a bottle of vodka on the table, and told him to sit down and have a talk with him.

"I never cared for you when you were engaged to my daughter, but I see now that my opinion of you was colored somewhat by my dislike for your grandmother. However, I see you differently now. Do you still love my daughter?"

Zyg answered that he had never stopped loving Elizabeth, which surprised him at the moment he uttered the words.

"Good. Then I give you my permission to marry my daughter. Take care of her."

Slowly he began disappearing before Zygmunt's eyes. The vision surprised and affected Zyg greatly . . . especially after his family received the letter from the Szelazek family and saw the funeral photos with Elizabeth among the mourners. The rest became history. Tadeusz had managed to bring happiness to his daughter, even after his death. His last unfinished task was completed posthumously. He left the family well taken care of, his contract with God was fulfilled, and the day of his death was of his own choosing. The prophecy of Symbolerus was completed.

≈ 36 ≈

Helena's Last Years

Keep God in your life.

Helena Szelazek had always lived for her family. Now that Tadeusz was gone, she dedicated her remaining years to giving support, encouragement, hope, and laughter to her children. She continuously showed her strength of character, especially in the moments that brought her close to death. It was courage and inner strength that got her through wars, starvation, illness, grief, and poverty.

Over the years, her hardships and illnesses had weakened her heart. X-rays revealed heart damage from undiagnosed, and untreated, heart attacks. A large area of her heart muscle was dead, and over time, she had had episodes of congestive heart failure and surgery to place stints in her arteries. There were painful angiograms, annoying oxygen equipment, and assorted hospital stays. Throughout all of this, she kept her serene outlook on life and a sense of humor, which entertained all the nurses and doctors alike. Perhaps it was because she had been in so many accidents throughout her lifetime that she began seeing the humor in it.

On April 15, 2000, Helena was relaxing in her living room watching television and peeling some radishes to eat with her lunch. The program she was watching was a science program that demonstrated how magnesium reacts when ignited. As she focused on the scene, her world exploded around her. A huge noise like an eruption was followed by the wall collapsing behind her. The wall was being pushed inward, moving her, along with the couch on which she was sitting, four feet toward the opposite wall. She sat there stunned, thinking, "Why would someone demolish my house just to demonstrate how explosive magnesium is? And what gave them the right to do that?"

The shock did not allow her brain to process the possibility that something else was occurring simultaneously. It was like watching virtual reality television with surround sound. This battle between reality and fantasy was probably what saved her from harm. Had she realized that a car had just plowed completely into her home, killing the two elderly ladies within it, she would have had a heart attack right then and there.

Apparently, the driver lost control of her car as she was traveling down the hill on Allen Street. She had either passed out (possibly from insulin shock since insurance records indicated that she had been a diabetic) or she had lost control of the car. She flew through the stop sign, through the hedge in the front yard (there were no indications that she even tried to apply the brakes as the vehicle bounced down the long front lawn of the yard), and straight into the house. The momentum wedged the car completely inside the spare bedroom, whereupon both women died upon impact.

Helena managed to crawl out of the window of her living room. Neighbors tried to assist her but she insisted that she was okay. She went back into the house and used the kitchen phone to call her daughters who immediately set out for the house with the rest of the family in tow. The police, ambulances, and fire department were already there when they arrived. The car was perched over the severed remains of a gas pipe that was still flowing. The gas heater unit was totally pushed out of the way, and it quickly became apparent that it was nothing short of a miracle that Helena had survived. The two front rooms were demolished; shards of cement, wood, glass, and plaster were wedged into the walls. Debris was scattered throughout the entire first floor apartment. Yet, despite being in the center of the crash and all of the rubble, Helena's injuries proved to be minor.

However, Helena was in a state of shock. Her right foot, right ankle, right knee, back, left shoulder, and the ribs on her left side had been injured. As the family began picking glass out of her hair, shoes, and clothing, they had an opportunity to explain to her what had really happened to her house. They did not tell her about the fate of the two women, hoping to spare her some additional stress.

She was taken to New Britain General Hospital . . . her least favorite hospital in the world. It always seemed that regardless of what she was being admitted for, they usually messed the procedures up. Nevertheless, as it was the closest hospital, the ambulance took her there. Helen told the emergency personnel that she was thirsty and experiencing pain; but no one allowed her to take any meds or to drink anything until they were ready to take x-rays—which didn't happen until nearly three hours had passed. It took them another hour to analyze the film. In the meantime, they hadn't even offered her an ice pack to help bring down the swelling and contusions.

The x-ray tech made her walk to the machine and stand up while they took the chest x-rays. No wheelchair was provided for her! They hadn't even determined if there was any internal bleeding or, if just by standing on her legs, she could be severing a vein or causing irreparable damage! One of the x-ray techs pushed her up against the x-ray machine, pressing hard against her injured back and shoulder. She screamed in pain, loud enough for everyone outside the door of the x-ray room to hear her. Even though Jadwiga tried to insist that she be allowed in with her mother, they did not allow her inside. They insisted that they spoke enough Polish to communicate with her. Obviously, Jadwiga should not have taken no for an answer.

Nearly five hours after entering the hospital, Helena was finally admitted. Her daughters did not leave her alone to endure the ministrations of the staff, and they took turns watching over her. Jadwiga spent the night sitting in a chair in her room, making sure no one made any mistakes on her meds or in any other procedure. This had become the pattern over the years. Her daughters couldn't risk her life from further clumsy nursing. (Just recently, a good friend of Helena's had been admitted to this hospital with chest pains. They had sent her home telling her it was nothing. The pain turned out to be a heart attack and the friend had died at home.)

The next day, which happened to be Palm Sunday, the nursing staff still did not know the full extent of Helena's injuries. The doctor (on call) told her that the x-rays showed no broken bones, and that the blood tests and urine specimens showed no internal damage, at least none that they could perceive. However, they did not take any MRI or CAT scans on which to base their opinions. Nevertheless, Helena was eager to leave the hospital regardless of what they felt was wrong with her. She was trying to convince her family to get her released before the hospital could find some way to kill her.

Oxygen tanks were delivered to Elizabeth's house, in anticipation of Helena's release from the hospital and for her extended stay with Elizabeth and Zygmunt. She needed to stay somewhere where she could get around-the-clock care, especially since she had no home to return to. Helena's house was totaled, but her family had already begun the process of reconstruction. Doug and Zyg sealed up the gaping hole in the front of the house with ply-wood after a tow truck pulled the car out of the building. After this, the long process of salvaging the contents of her house and her life began.

Helena was discharged the next day. (Elizabeth and Zyg had already set up a twin bed for her in their first-floor living room, and over the following months, they took exceptional care of her.) When they finally got her into Elizabeth's house, she was exhausted and in pain. As Jadwiga carefully removed her sweater, she found that the nursing staff at New Britain General had failed to remove the IV hook-up tube from her arm. Jadwiga had no choice but to remove the IV herself since she had no intentions of dragging their exhausted mother back to the hospital. This was yet another example of the inattentive care that was given to patients at that facility.

Eventually, the family found out why Helena was still in pain despite the fact that the hospital had given her a clean bill of health. On April 26, Helena went in for an appointment at the V.A. Hospital in Newington with her general care physician, Elaine Sweat. Her family had been waiting anxiously for this appointment to have her checked out properly. Her chest and side were still hurting her and her foot was still swollen. Her doctor found an infection on the top of her injured foot where the skin had been pierced by a shard of glass. Then she prescribed an oral antibiotic and a series of x-rays. The x-ray films confirm what they all suspected—three fractured ribs. Her knee was bruised, but was mending, and the swollen foot had soft tissue damage. Still, for a woman of 82, she did very well living through an accident of that magnitude. Helena was extremely lucky to have had such minor injuries.

What bothered Helena most about the accident was the death of the two ladies. She was acquainted with both of them. Tadeusz had worked with both of their husbands at the factory and they all had acquaintances in common. It was much harder for Helena not to dwell on the deaths of those two women when their faces kept coming to her mind. They were not nameless, faceless strangers to her. She had often invited them to visit her and to drop in whenever they had the time. Helena hadn't quite expected them to drop into her house in this particular manner.

The house on Farmington Avenue was in shambles and required extensive reconstruction work. The family all pitched in to help. Jadwiga also handled the other issues that arose from the accident—medical, financial, legal, insurance-related, and so on. She knew that she had a limited timeframe within which to complete the restoration of her family home and to help her mother get back to her normal life. Jadwiga was fighting against the clock because her family of four was already in the process of moving to Hawaii. It had been determined, after Doug's second open heart surgery in January, that he would be healthier living in the mild climate of Hawaii, and they were planning the move for July. He needed to take an early retirement to extend his life. The thought of leaving her mother tore her apart, but her obligations to her husband and children took precedence. Helena understood that it was necessary for her daughter to make the move for her family's sake. She told Jadwiga that she would visit someday, if her health permitted. Jadwiga's greatest fear was that that day would never happen.

Helena did end up visiting the Big Island of Hawaii in 2001, as it turned out. Her daughter and family were delighted to see her again because Jadwiga had been uncertain if Helena should even undertake such a long trip. Her health problems made the plane ride even more difficult and uncomfortable. The oxygen tanks, which her daughter had requested to help her breathe, were placed on the floor under her feet. This placement made it very uncomfortable for her during the 12-hour trip from Connecticut to Hawaii. Despite the fact that she was traveling first class, this trip still made huge demands upon her strength.

Once she recovered from her ordeal, Helena loved the island with its warmth, beauty, and strange plants. Her joy at being in such a gracious, warm community of people was a pleasure to see. The Hawaiian people, in turn, loved her. She made friends with the ladies at the Veterans Administration in Kona, and they helped provide her with a free wheelchair, oxygen, and medication during her stay. This made it easy for her family to wheel her through the beautiful parks and streets of Hawaii.

Helena loved the quaint chapels, the small missionary houses, and all of the local Hawaiian legends of gods and goddesses. She especially loved St. Michael's church in Kona, with all the people wearing leis and flowers as they attended mass. She told us that this was the first church where she felt everyone truly cared for each other as they held hands, sang, prayed, and hugged each other. She even met one of her VA ladies in church. The warm greeting that she extended to Helena made her feel at home and part of the community. It was at St. Michael's that she had the opportunity to meet, and speak with, the Catholic bishop of the Hawaiian Islands as he performed a mass at the small church. She found out that he had once lived in Connecticut. After a pleasant conversation with her, he gave her a warm hug, and posed for a photo with her.

Helena delighted in the beauty of the flowers, waterfalls, and inspiring scenery of the Big Island. Her daughter's home was a beautiful structure located in the Kona Heavens district with a magnificent view overlooking the west coast of Kona. The garden was filled with fruit trees, palms, pools, and a waterfall with a Koi pond. Her daughter and family wanted nothing more than to keep her with them forever. On the day she was to leave the island, Helena stood for a while looking in the direction of the airport.

"Now I know how to fly here after I die, so that I can, once again, visit those I love most dearly."

This was to be her last visit with her daughter and it was her last major excursion to distant parts of the world. Yet, Jadwiga knew she did visit again in spirit because she felt Helena's presence many times during the following years.

Elizabeth and Zyg had taken over Helena's care after Jadwiga left Connecticut. Zygmunt would drive her to most of her doctor's appointments and they kept an eye on her slowly failing health. The nursing staff at the VA hospital assumed that Zyg was her son because of the concerned, attentive care he gave her during her checkups. He had always felt close to Helena, ever since his own childhood. His mother (Grazyna Kacicki) was the daughter of Halina Podlasek—the same Podlaseks who sponsored the Szelazeks. Helena often babysat Zyg, his brother, and sister after they moved to Connecticut from Canada. The Szelazek girls immediately accepted him as their brother. He even went through a finger-cutting, blood-brother pact with Elizabeth and Jadwiga when he was eight, even though the girls didn't think much of his bravery. This was because he was too squeamish to cut his own finger! The three children were inseparable from the start. In many ways, he was more Helena's son than his own mother's—and this is something that Zyg still has trouble reconciling. When he had to make a choice between caring for Helena during her last year of life and visiting his mother in Arizona during her battle with cancer, he chose to be with Helena. This caused the Szelazek sisters to wonder on several occasions if there was some connection between the son my mother lost, Jurek, and Zyg, who eventually became her son-in-law. Remember, Jurek died in England of intestinal problems in 1947; Zyg was born in England in 1949 with a closed pyloric valve, an intestinal condition that had to be repaired by cutting open his stomach valve where it meets the small intestine. This had to be done within days of his birth or he would have died. The close bond he always had with

Helena could possibly be more intricate than conventional explanations can offer.

During her final years, Helena still tended her gardens, drove to church, attended her veterans' meetings, and kept her own finances in order. Despite her weakened state, she always had a positive attitude, which had a great influence on her family's morale. She had a way of turning their serious problems into bearable situations through her jokes, sense of humor, and her very presence. They always felt that so long as she was around, everything would work out alright. There would be many dark clouds looming over the future horizons of her children; but while she lived, everything was contained, safe, and hopeful.

Eventually, Dr. Borkowski, Helena's cardiologist, had some difficulty adjusting her medication. Her cardiac problems were severe and there was extensive damage to heart tissue. So, to assist the functioning of her heart, he suggested a pacemaker. Helena was worried that this would be the final surgery of her life, but she understood the necessity of trying to improve the quality of her life. An acquaintance of hers had just had one installed and it had worked out well for her. Therefore, Helena decided to undergo the surgery. A surgeon was chosen for the implant and the procedure was schedule for Monday, December 9, 2002, in New Britain General Hospital. She would have preferred any other hospital, but the surgeon was on staff at this facility. She made it through the operation and seemed okay at first. However, she soon felt that her heart was beating too forcefully. You could actually see the pounding of her heart in her chest and she seemed to be more tired than usual. In the doctor's office, the nurse had difficulty drawing blood from her veins. The nurse made a huge bruise on her wrist when they were unable to locate a useable vein in her arm. The blood did not want to fill the bottle, and it seemed thick and sluggish. This abnormality worried Helena.

That night, she awoke from a dream about being chased and eaten by coyotes. Her heart was pounding within her, and she knew something was wrong. The next morning, the doctor who performed the implant decided to lower the intensity of the pacemaker. She was again admitted to the hospital on Friday, the 13th of December. The surgeon made the adjustment; however, he and the hospital made a grave error. Instead of monitoring her condition overnight and decreasing the intensity in stages, they sent her home that same afternoon.

Elizabeth usually spent Friday nights with Helena to keep an eye on her. It had become a Friday night custom to bring along Elizabeth's adopted grandchildren, a good movie to watch, and a good supper. Then they would all spend the night together. However, this Friday night was different. After her release from the hospital, Helena tried to draw a drop of blood from her finger for her daily diabetes testing, but she was unable to get her finger to bleed. This caused Elizabeth much concern but Helena said to just leave it alone; she had had enough of doctors, hospitals, and needles. She would go see them next week if necessary. So, that evening, Elizabeth entertained her as best as she could.

Liz finally helped Helena into bed that night, and they had just fallen asleep, when Helena's old black cat, Kitchkey, began to howl for no apparent reason. He was making horrifying sounds, screaming with fear as he jumped off her bed and ran to hide himself among the sleeping children. His fur was standing on end, and his tail was puffed out in fear. Helena asked Liz, "Do you think he sees my death?"

The Szelazek family had always believed that animals could see death, as it waited for the final moments of life to end, so this wasn't a strange statement to Elizabeth. She tried to downplay her mother's fears by saying that the old cat didn't see anything. She called it an old wives' tale, just stupid stuff to make you scared. She then talked about other subjects, trying to cheer Helena up, despite the cold chill she was feeling in her heart. She talked about all of the sisters' families, children, grandchildren, and plans for the future. The topic came up about how jealous people still were of Helena's life, even after all of these difficult years. Just that week, an acquaintance of Helena's told her that she looked too good for someone who was supposedly having heart problems. It was this type of jealousy that had been the cause of much unhappiness in Helena's life. People seemed to covet whatever she had and whatever small good befell her—even though there was nothing to be jealous of. Elizabeth assured her that all of that didn't matter anymore, none of those people mattered. She told her that she was proud and honored to have been her daughter in this lifetime, and she would never have chosen anyone else for a mother if she were given a choice in the matter. They kissed each other good night and then Helena went to sleep.

Elizabeth finally fell asleep later that night. She heard Helena get up once during the night, to relieve herself, before going back to sleep again. Elizabeth checked on her and found her sleeping quietly. Early in the morning, she came into the room to check on her. Helena's chest was still slightly warm to the touch, but Elizabeth could no longer detect a heartbeat. Her body was lying in a peaceful state, eyes just slightly open, with an angelic expression on her face. She had died in her sleep . . . peacefully, and nobly. There was no visible trauma, no pain, and no convulsions. Helena Semerylo Szelazek died on December 14, 2002, ten years after her beloved Tadeusz had passed away.

The family gathered around her bed and said a rosary while the ambulance personnel notified the funeral home. The director of the New Britain Memorial Funeral Home, Anna Targonski, arrived personally to handle all the details. She had been a good friend to Helena and was determined to help in any way possible. Elizabeth called Jadwiga in Hawaii and she took the first flight out to be with everyone during the final preparations for her mother's burial. Jadwiga had taken the last seat on a flight out of Kona and had arrived in Connecticut the next day, the day after her mother's death. Jadwiga prepared the final copy of the obituary and helped with all of the final details. The family arranged the wake, church ceremony, and the gathering at the Veterans' hall. Krystyna helped organize the specifics of the mass and the choices of choir music for the church service.

Elizabeth and Jadwiga made final choices on the printed notices, memorial prayer cards, and flowers, but they still needed to choose a casket. So, Anna, the funeral director, led them downstairs to the basement display room to show them the various models available. The last time Elizabeth had been down there was when she and Helena had chosen a casket for Tadeusz. As they walked through the area, Elizabeth touched each casket and both sisters wondered out loud what kind of casket she would like. She had simple tastes and disliked ostentatious extravagance. Helena had chosen a simple oak casket for her Tadeusz, so her daughters knew her preferences. They knew that she liked soft pillows under her head and warm covers on her legs when she slept.

As they walked through the room, Elizabeth said that she wished Helena could help them decide which one she wanted. She walked up to a simple oak casket with a soft white pillow, which Anna identified as the model that Helena bought for Tadeusz. As Elizabeth touched the surface of the casket, she asked Helena if this was the one. All the lights went out in the downstairs area, leaving the group in darkness. Within a minute the lights went back on. Anna called upstairs to ask if someone had shut down any lights in the building and they said no. Nowhere else had the lights gone dead—just the area where the sisters were standing. The first thing Anna said when she joined the other two was, "I guess your mother visited us." This was exactly what Elizabeth and Jadwiga had been thinking. So, the decision was made for them, and they picked the casket that Helena had chosen.

On the day before the wake, the sisters visited with a friend of Jadwiga's who lived in the vicinity. The friend, Mrs. Pylak, had always possessed the gift of "sight" and had often told Jadwiga things before they happened. She had always been forthright in her beliefs, very spiritual in nature, and usually accurate in her pronouncements. She was sought out by the clergy to give comfort to the sick and the dying. She had also worked with detectives to help locate missing persons. Mrs. Pylak extended her sympathies to the Szelazek family upon the passing of Helena. She then told Elizabeth and Jadwiga that Helena was still near them and that she wanted each one of her loved ones to receive a different memento from her belongings. Mrs. Pylak specifically, and accurately, described Helena's favorite prayer book, her rosary from Bethlehem, and certain framed photos on Helena's wall. Then Mrs. Pylak said, "Your mother is trying to show me something about her hands. She keeps covering her left hand with her right hand as though she wants to cover something up. And then she is taking her hair and pushing it up over to the left side of her head. I'm not sure what she means, but she indicates that you will understand."

It immediately dawned on them that Helena was embarrassed by the ugly black bruise on her wrist and hand where the needle had punctured a vein. A nurse had created the disfigurement earlier that week while drawing blood. She wanted that defect covered by her good hand and she wanted them to know it. So the sisters decided, then and there, to put a small corsage of pink roses on her wrist. The other hand would hold a rosary. As for the significance of moving her hair around, the sisters weren't sure what that meant; but they felt that they'd find out soon enough. On the way home, they stopped by and told Anna to be sure and make the appropriate changes and to place her hands in the correct placement.

On the afternoon of the wake, they arrived early at the funeral home. Helena was clothed in a pastel, sea-foam green dress that she had especially chosen for this occasion. It made her look elegant . . . like royalty. When her daughters saw her lying on her soft pillow, they found out what the second part of her special request was all about. They saw that the makeup technician had parted her hair on the wrong side of her head and had given her little bangs. It had always been a strong preference of Helena's to part her hair only on the right side and never on the left. She also disliked bangs and felt they did not suit her face. Hairdressers were not allowed to make that error while styling her hair. If they did, she would always change the part in her hair as soon as she got home. So, standing over her casket, her daughters quickly grabbed a comb, a can of hairspray, and corrected the error that Helena had brought to their attention. Even in death, a woman has the right to look good.

A Scottish piper played the bagpipes for her at the church and the cemetery. This was very appropriate since the Scottish people had always held a warm spot in her heart. Ever since they had teamed up with Scotsmen in the British Army during WWII, and then again when they had lived among them in Great Britain, Helena and Tadeusz always held them in high esteem. So, hearing the pipes at her funeral was truly fitting.

The family displayed Helena's war medals on a red velvet heart-shaped pillow and draped both the Polish and American flags across her coffin before her burial, to show her allegiance to the country of her birth and the country of her chosen home. The veterans honored her that day with a full military 21-gun salute at the cemetery. Jadwiga gave a short eulogy in Polish and English, telling all those present about what Helena's greatest gift to the world was:

"When Tadeusz moved into a new town in Poland, he attended church services at a small village church. He heard an angelic soprano voice in the choir and looking up, he saw a blond-haired, blue-eyed angel. He immediately fell in love and married her. She filled our lives with joy, and every occasion was a fitting opportunity to share her gift of song with us. She offered her voice to God, from whom all gifts and blessings arise. So, in her honor, my sisters and I will sing for her one more time."

Helena and Tadeusz Szelazek

They sang "Jak Szybko Mijaja Chwile (How Quickly Pass the Moments)." The mourners all joined in, singing the moving words, as they all remembered how quickly they would all be leaving this world. "… A year, a day, a moment… no longer will we be together."

With Helena's passing, the final chapters of the Szelazek family's journey to Eden came to a close. The predictions of Symbolerus were completed. All the lessons that Tadeusz and Helena had taught their children were left for them to understand, to follow, and to teach to future generations.

They showed their daughters that no one knows the full extent of their own capabilities; and that sometimes it is tragedy and loss that brings out the greatest strength within us . . . the greatest accomplishments. What we are destined to do in the future lies within our individual fates . . . predestined, but flexible. Their story continues in the lives of their children, grandchildren, and even their great grandchildren. Hopefully, these generations of Szelazek descendants will also lead lives of nobility and honor—as exemplary as the lives of Tadeusz and Helena. Perhaps future generations might even exceed the deeds of their fathers and forefathers. The story will never end while their spirits are still alive within each of us.

Memories

As lights are dimmed, and sounds are muted . . .
When visions are our only company . . .
At the end of the day, as time is stilled . . .
All that's left is our memory.

Worthless are the clothes we wear.
Worthless are the coins we count.
Worthless are the cures for things . . .
That ail our lives so constantly.

Gone our youth of false pretenses.
Gone the jobs defining worth.
Gone the world imbued with lies . . .
Earning Karma sealed at birth.

From dying lips we hear refrains . . .
The essence of what life remains . . .
Above yourself, place Love and those,
Who help you keep the memories close.

By Jadwiga Szelazek Morrison
2009

Epilogue

There are few questions in our lives as important as "When does conscious life end?" "Can the deceased communicate with the living?" "How can we rejoin those who have died before us?" I can only present the events and facts of our lives as answers or evidence.

There have been several interesting incidents since the death of our parents, Helena and Tadeusz Szelazek. One has to do with the oak box that contains the war medals, documents, and flags belonging to both of them. These objects meant a great deal to our parents during their lifetime, so we placed them in this heavy, decorative, latched box. It is impossible to pry open the lid without physically unlatching it. And yet, on several occasions, we have found it unlatched and slightly ajar. The latest "opening" occurred recently, on February 2, 2010, coincidentally on the anniversary of Helena and Tadeusz's wedding. With these incidents, they have let us know that they are with us, that they are still conscious of those things that mattered in their former lifetimes, and that they love us.

Another incident occurred five days after our mother died. Elizabeth knew that mom had felt reluctant in promising us that she would visit after her death. We all remembered how Helena had felt, as a child, when her dearest grandfather was dying. The adults had always frightened children with ghost and grim reaper stories, and that had kept her away from his bedside. Therefore, Helena was worried that perhaps she would inadvertently frighten us if she were to appear unannounced. She was never convinced that we would look forward to a visit from her. Liz's son, Adam, had already experienced her presence a few days earlier, when he had been talking about how much he missed his grandmother. He was standing near the porch light in his home when it had popped and burnt out, letting him know that she was there. Other members of the family had had dreams about her and had felt her presence. That Thursday morning (December 19, 2002), Liz was lying on her bed when she felt little electric kisses starting on her right cheek, past her mouth, over to her left cheek, and then back to her lips. There was a golden, warm glow all around her, and it gave her such a feeling of overwhelming joy and peace. It was a feeling she had never experienced before—complete and utter happiness. She felt Helena telling her that she was okay. "Don't cry anymore; I'm happy." Then the light began to fade and her presence left the room. Liz knew she had just been visited by Helena because the very fact that she was feeling such happiness during the worst time of her life, indicated that her mother was there, trying to cheer her up.

We believe that loving relationships made during our lifetimes create an anchor that keeps us connected with each other after death. Strong emotions, like love, create an electrical bond between souls, thus allowing them to interact in this lifetime and the next. By keeping the memory of those we have lost fresh in our hearts and minds, we strengthen that connection. Everything we do to keep them close, like prayer, meditation, dreams, and interpreting synchronistic events or messages, strengthens this bond or connection. We all hope that a time will come soon, when conventional science will verify that which we can only sense as truth . . . perhaps it will even assist us in communicating with those who left us behind. After all, once upon a time, television was just a magical concept . . . grabbing images from the air.

Bibliography

Video

Szmagier, Krzysztof. *Bo Wolnosc Krzyzami sie mierzy* (General Anders).

Reference Books

Linde, M. S. B. *Slownik Jezyka Polskiego.* Lwow, Poland, Zakladu Ossolinskich Press, 1859.

Mosby's Medical Dictionary, eighth edition, Elsevier, Mosby Imprint, 2008.

Books

Hagerty, Barbara B. *Fingerprints of God: The Search for the Science of Spirituality.* New York, Riverhead Books, 2009.

Kalkowski, Tadeusz. *Tysiac Lat Monety Polskiej.* Krakow, Poland, Wydawnictwo Literackie, 1981.

Powell, Diane Hennacy. *The ESP Enigma: The Scientific Case for Psychic Phenomena.* New York, Walker & Company, 2008.

Sword, Keith. Deportation and Exile: Poles in the Soviet Union, 1939–48. London, UK, St. Martin's Press, 1994.

Periodicals

Cayce, Edward. Reading 5752-2 on psychic development, from various readings and psychic documents (Association for Research and Enlightenment, Virginia Beach, VA). Access online at are-cayce.org/ecreadings.

Documents on Polish Soviet Relations (DPSR). (Vol.1, London, 1961) p. 68.

Stephey, M.J. "The Science Behind Psychic Phenomena," *Time Science Magazine*, (Dec.24, 2008.) Search time.com.

About the Author

Jadwiga Morrison, or Jadzia (Yah-Jah) for short, lives in Burlington, Connecticut where she teaches in the Special Services Department of the regional high school. She received her Liberal Arts degree in English from Central Connecticut State University with a minor in History. After living in Hawaii for a number of years, she returned to Connecticut where she has been writing and working on various literary projects. Her next literary project, titled *This Life of Mine*, is a book of illustrated poetry inspired by real-life truths.

Jadwiga is also a certified Transpersonal Hypnotherapist (CHt) specializing in helping people with various compulsions, phobias, bad habits, and learning disabilities.

COMBINING HISTORY AND HARDSHIP, betrayal and disease, miraculous escapes, and death-defying encounters, *From Exile to Eden* chronicles one family's journey from deportation to Siberia to freedom in America.

In *From Exile to Eden,* **Jadwiga Szelazek Morrison** traces her family's harrowing yet inspirational flight from war-torn Europe beginning with two remarkable people—**Tadeusz Szelazek** and **Helena Semerylo.** Add in adventure, romance, parapsychology—this epic family saga, based on memoirs and family journals, took several decades to compile. It is a story well worth telling, and well worth waiting for.

Helena Semerylo was born on Armistice Day 1918. Her psychic awakening began at the age of five when she was struck by lightning. Her abilities, which proved to be both a blessing and a curse to her and her family, led her on a journey to distant lands far from the land of her birth. **Tadeusz Szelazek** was born into a titled family of the old Polish aristocracy. He followed a path of intellectual pursuits with which he tried to unravel the meaning of life; he found the answers within himself and his family. A chance encounter with a world-renown seer left him in possession of predictions concerning his future. With logic and intellect battling the possibilities of predestination, he found his life unfolding in patterns which he fought to control and change… to no avail.

Together the two create an unforgettable tale of love, loyalty, courage, and inspiration.

ISBN: 978-1-61852-040-1   U.S. $23.95

5 2 3 9 5

9 781618 520401